Thriving After Loss

A Compassionate Guide to Healing, Identity, and Living Fully Again

By Ceaira Harris

Ceaira K Publishing

Published by
Ceaira K Publishing

© 2026 Ceaira K Publishing. All rights reserved.

No part of this publication may be reproduced, distributed, or transmitted in any form or by any means, including photocopying, recording, or other electronic or mechanical methods, without the prior written permission of the publisher, except in the case of brief quotations embodied in reviews and certain other noncommercial uses permitted by copyright law.

This book is intended for informational and inspirational purposes only. It is not intended to replace professional advice.

ISBN: 979-8-950179-00-6

Cover design by: Ceaira K Publishing
Interior design by: Ceaira K Publishing

Printed in the United States of America

Dedication

To my children,

You have lived through moments no child should have to face, and still, you continue to grow, love, and show up in ways that inspire me every day.

This book was written from a place of loss, but also from a place of love—and so much of that love lives on through you.

You carry your father's presence in ways words can't fully explain, and because of that, he is never far from us.

You remind me that even in the hardest seasons, there is still life, still meaning, and still a reason to keep going.

I love you more than words could ever fully express.

This book is also dedicated to everyone who has loved deeply and lost.

To those carrying grief quietly.
To those learning how to breathe again.
To those rebuilding their lives in pieces.

To the parents, partners, children, friends, and caregivers.
To those grieving humans, pets, relationships, identities, and dreams.
To those surviving in ways no one sees.

And to those who feel unseen in their healing.

May these pages remind you that your pain matters,
your life still holds meaning,
and you are allowed to become something new.

You are not alone.

Author's Note

I didn't meet grief just once in my life. It came to me in waves. It showed up early, through abandonment, loss, instability, and moments that asked me to grow up faster than I should have. It continued into adulthood in many forms — pregnancy loss, family deaths, illness, sudden violence, widowhood, and the quieter grief that follows when relationships change and life no longer looks the way it once did. Some losses were loud. Some were silent. Some were expected. Some arrived without warning. Over time, I learned that grief doesn't only happen after death. We grieve people and pets, homes and relationships, versions of ourselves, dreams that didn't unfold the way we imagined, along with safety and stability.

Grief doesn't always announce itself. Sometimes it shows up as exhaustion. Sometimes as anxiety. Sometimes as numbness. Sometimes as survival mode. For a long time, I didn't realize how much I was carrying. I functioned. I showed up. I kept going. But surviving and living are not the same. Somewhere along the way, I made a quiet decision: I didn't want grief to define my life. I wanted to learn how to live fully again — not by erasing what I had lost, but by learning how to carry it differently.

This book isn't written from theory. It's written from lived experience. From rebuilding myself more than once. From learning how to breathe again after loss. And if you're holding this book right now, I want you to know something important: you don't have to rush your healing. You don't have to pretend you're okay. And you don't have to walk this alone.

Why I Wrote This Book

I wrote this book because too many people are surviving silently. They wake up every day carrying grief in their bodies, in their thoughts, in their routines — and no one teaches them how to move forward without abandoning what they've lost. Most grief resources focus on coping. This book focuses on thriving. Not pretending everything is okay. Not bypassing pain. But gently learning how to rebuild mentally, emotionally, physically, spiritually, financially, and relationally. I wrote this because grief doesn't just affect emotions — it affects sleep, energy, decision-making, relationships, money, and even your sense of identity. And yet, so many people are left to figure all of that out alone.

I also wrote this book to normalize support. Your support system often includes more than you might realize — family, friends, therapists, doctors, spiritual leaders, support groups, online communities, coworkers, neighbors, even pets. Support doesn't have to look perfect. It just has to exist. And if your support system feels small right now, this book is part of it. I wrote this because grief is not weakness — it is evidence of love. And thriving after loss is not betrayal — it is courage. You are allowed to want joy again. You are allowed to build a meaningful life. You are allowed to experience abundance after grief. This book is here to walk with you as you do.

Table Of Contents

Table Of Contents

Introduction

The only guarantee of life is death. That may sound heavy, but it's also honest. Loss is woven into being human. Every person who lives long enough will grieve something — someone they love, a season of life, a relationship, a dream, a sense of safety, or even a part of themselves. Grief doesn't discriminate. It doesn't care about age, income, culture, or background. And yet, even though it's universal, grief often feels incredibly lonely. You can be surrounded by people and still feel completely alone inside your pain. Sometimes it feels like no one truly understands what you're carrying.

That's why this book exists. Not to fix you. Not to rush your healing. Not to tell you how long grief should last. This book exists to sit beside you — to help you understand what you're experiencing, to offer practical tools, and to remind you that thriving is still possible, even after loss. You can use this book alongside therapy, or let it stand on its own. You don't have to read it in order. You don't have to relate to every chapter. Everything here won't apply to everyone, but there is something in these pages for every person.

This is a book for those grieving loved ones, pets, relationships, identities, stability, or versions of life that no longer exist. It's for every situation and every stage of grief. Sometimes I'm writing to you. Sometimes I'm writing to myself. Because healing isn't a destination — it's a practice. And thriving doesn't mean you stop missing what you lost. It means you learn how to live again while carrying it.

PART ONE: GRIEF IS PART OF BEING HUMAN

Chapter 1

The Only Guarantee of Life Is Death

"Grief doesn't arrive because you are weak. It arrives because you loved."

There's one truth we all share, whether we talk about it or not: the only guarantee of life is death. Not success. Not happiness. Not stability. Not longevity. Loss is woven into the human experience. From the moment we begin forming attachments, we also begin risking heartbreak. We love people. We care for pets. We nurture plants. We build homes. We create routines. We imagine futures. We attach meaning to moments. And eventually, something changes. Someone leaves. Someone dies. Something ends. Something breaks. Something shifts. Grief doesn't arrive because you are weak — it arrives because you loved, because you cared, because something mattered.

Yet most of us grow up without ever learning how to grieve. We're taught how to achieve, how to work, how to be productive — but we're rarely taught how to sit with loss. So when grief comes, and it always does, it can feel overwhelming, confusing, and deeply isolating. You may find yourself wondering why it hurts this much, why you feel exhausted all the time, why your mind feels foggy, or why everything suddenly feels heavier than it should. These aren't signs that something is wrong with you. They're signs that your nervous system is processing loss.

When we lose someone or something we're attached to, the brain responds as if we're in danger. This isn't weakness — it's biology. Attachment lives deep in the nervous system. It's how humans bond, survive, and connect. So when that bond is broken, the body goes on alert. Stress hormones rise. Sleep changes. Concentration drops. Emotions feel heavier. You may feel foggy, exhausted, or disconnected. This is your system trying to protect you, not punish you. Research even shows that grief activates the same areas of the brain associated with physical pain, which is why loss can feel unbearable in your chest, your stomach, or your whole body. You're not imagining this. You're experiencing it.

Grief isn't just emotional — it lives in your body. It shows up in your sleep, affects your appetite, clouds your thoughts, changes your energy, and alters your sense of safety. Sometimes grief is loud, arriving as tears, anger, or despair. Sometimes it's quiet, showing up as numbness, fatigue, or withdrawal. Sometimes it comes in waves. Sometimes it appears out of nowhere, stirred by a smell, a song, a place, or a memory. And sometimes it doesn't announce itself at all. It hides behind productivity. It hides behind busyness. It hides behind strength.

Many people don't even realize they're grieving because their loss doesn't look like what society labels as grief. But grief isn't only about death. We grieve relationships that ended. We grieve childhoods we didn't get. We grieve versions of ourselves that no longer exist. We grieve financial security, health, dreams, and safety. We grieve pets and plants — living beings we nurtured, bonded with, and loved. Those bonds matter. Loss is loss. There is no hierarchy of grief. Your pain doesn't need to be compared to anyone else's to be valid. If it hurts, it matters.

Grief can feel especially isolating because of the cultures we grow up in. Some cultures mourn openly. Some encourage silence and strength. Some ritualize loss. Some move quickly past it. Some avoid it altogether. So depending on how you were raised, you may have learned to suppress your feelings, stay busy, or "be strong" instead of letting yourself feel what hurts. That can make grief feel even lonelier. You may look around and think everyone else is moving forward while you feel stuck. But grief is deeply personal. Two people can experience the same loss and feel completely different inside. There is no correct way to grieve. There is only your way.

One of the hardest parts of grief is how alone it can make you feel. Invisible. Misunderstood. Left behind. But grief is universal. Every person you pass on the street is carrying something. Some carry visible loss. Some carry invisible loss. Some carry grief they've never processed. Some carry grief so old they've forgotten where it began. You are not alone in this experience, even when it feels deeply personal.

And here's something important: grief is not something you "get over." It's something you learn to carry. But how you carry it matters. You can carry grief in a way that slowly drains your life, or you can learn to carry it in a way that allows you to live fully again. That doesn't mean forgetting what you lost. It means learning how to honor it while still choosing life.

This book isn't here to minimize your pain. It's here to help you understand it, normalize it, and gently support you. It's here to remind you that surviving is not the same as living. Thriving doesn't mean pretending everything is okay. Thriving means learning how to rebuild. It means finding moments of peace again. It means allowing joy to coexist with sadness. It means discovering who you are becoming through what you've endured.

And wherever you are right now — angry, numb, overwhelmed, heartbroken, or simply tired — you are exactly where you're allowed to be. You don't need permission to feel what you feel. You don't have to rush this. There is no timeline for grief. There is only your process. Take a breath. You are still here. And that matters.

I want you to take some time to reflect on your life right now.

Take a moment to sit with this question:

What loss am I carrying right now?

Write whatever comes up. There is no right or wrong answer.

Let's complete this quick but gentle practice.

Place one hand on your chest.

Take three slow breaths.

Say quietly (or in your mind):
> *I am allowed to feel this.*
> *I am allowed to take my time.*
> *I am still becoming.*

Come back to this practice anytime you feel you need or want to.

Chapter 2

What Grief Really Is

"If it mattered to you, it matters here. Every loss deserves compassion."

Grief is often misunderstood. Most people think it only happens after someone dies, but grief is much bigger than that. Grief is the emotional, physical, mental, and spiritual response to the loss of attachment — to anything that once gave you meaning, comfort, identity, safety, or connection. It's what happens when something that mattered is no longer the same. Sometimes that loss arrives suddenly. Sometimes it unfolds slowly. Sometimes it's obvious, and sometimes it's invisible. But all of it counts.

Grief lives in many places at once. Emotionally, it might show up as sadness, anger, guilt, numbness, anxiety, or longing. Physically, it can feel like fatigue, tightness in your chest, headaches, stomach discomfort, changes in appetite, or disrupted sleep. Mentally, it may bring brain fog, forgetfulness, racing thoughts, difficulty concentrating, or memories that replay on a loop. Spiritually, it can shake your sense of meaning, faith, purpose, or connection to something greater than yourself. And sometimes grief doesn't feel dramatic at all. Sometimes it feels quiet. Heavy. Subtle. Like something inside you shifted and never fully returned to how it was. That is grief too.

The Grief We Don't Talk About

There is also hidden grief — the kind that doesn't always come with a funeral or public acknowledgment. It lives in the quieter losses: the loss of identity, routine, safety, independence, financial stability, health, dreams, or even the version of life you thought you were building. This kind of grief often goes unnoticed, sometimes even by the person carrying it. You might tell yourself, *It's not that bad,* or *Others have it worse.* You might remind yourself to be grateful, or feel pressure to stay strong.

But minimizing your grief doesn't make it disappear. It simply teaches your body to hold it quietly. And quiet grief still takes up space.

What you're feeling matters — even when it doesn't have a name, a ceremony, or anyone else witnessing it.

All Grief Counts

We grieve people — parents, partners, children, friends, and family members. But grief doesn't stop there. We also grieve pets, who offer unconditional love, companionship, routine, and emotional safety. We grieve plants and gardens — living things we nurture, care for, and watch grow. We grieve homes that hold memories and identity. We grieve relationships, even when they end for necessary reasons. We grieve health when our bodies no longer function the way they once did. We grieve financial stability when security disappears. We grieve identity when life changes who we are.

These losses matter.

Psychology shows that humans form deep emotional bonds with animals, and for many people, pets truly are family. They provide comfort, consistency, and emotional regulation, which is why losing them can activate the same grief responses as losing a human loved one. Grieving a pet is real grief. And grieving a plant or garden can be real grief too — especially when it represents nurturing, stability, growth, or connection to nature.

You may feel silly admitting that out loud. But attachment is attachment. Loss is loss.

There is no hierarchy of grief. There is no "small" loss when something mattered to you.

Removing shame from grief is part of healing. You don't have to justify why something hurts. If it affected your life, your body, your heart, or your sense of safety — it counts.

Why Grief Doesn't Look the Same for Everyone

Two people can experience the same loss and respond in completely different ways. One person may cry openly, while another shuts down. One may talk constantly, and another goes quiet. One may feel intense sadness right away, while another feels numb at first. All of this is normal.

Your grief is shaped by so many things — your past experiences, your attachment style, your nervous system, your culture, your support system, your personality, and even the responsibilities you're carrying right now. Some people grew up with safe spaces to express emotions. Others learned to survive by staying quiet. Some were taught to be strong. Some were taught to feel freely.

In psychology, this is understood as individual grief expression — there is no universal template for how loss should be processed.

There is no correct way to grieve.

There is only your way.

And whatever your way looks like right now, it is allowed.

You Don't Have to Earn Your Grief

You don't need a dramatic story for your pain to matter. You don't need permission to feel what you feel, and you don't need to compare your loss to anyone else's or prove that it was "bad enough." Grief isn't a competition — it's a human experience. And like every human experience that touches the heart, it deserves compassion. Whatever brought you here is enough. Whatever you're carrying is valid.

Take some time to do this important exercise: Naming Your Losses

Take a few moments with this.

You don't need to rush. You don't need to be perfect.

Simply write down what comes to mind.

Ask yourself:

What people have I lost?
What animals have I lost?
What routines, identities, or versions of myself have changed?
What dreams or expectations no longer exist?
What sense of safety or stability has shifted?

Write freely.

You may be surprised by what surfaces. Some losses may feel big. Some may feel quiet. All of them matter.

Naming your losses is not about reopening wounds. It's about acknowledging what your body and heart already know.

Healing begins with honesty.

Let's complete this quick but gentle practice.

Place one hand on your heart.

Take a slow breath.

Say quietly:

My grief is real.
My losses matter.
I am allowed to take up space in my healing.

Come back to this practice anytime you feel you need or want to.

Chapter 3

The Myth of "Getting Over It"

"You don't get over grief. You learn how to carry it while still choosing life."

One of the most painful expectations placed on people who are grieving is the idea that you should eventually "get over it," as if grief has an expiration date, as if healing means forgetting, as if loving deeply should come with a timeline. Let me say this clearly: healing is not forgetting. You don't get over loss — you learn how to carry it. Grief doesn't disappear just because time passes. It changes shape. It softens in some places and resurfaces in others. Over time, it becomes part of your life story. And that doesn't mean something is wrong with you. It means you are human. So if you've ever wondered why waves of sadness still show up months or even years later, you're not failing at healing. You're experiencing attachment — your nervous system remembering what mattered.

What's Actually Happening in Your Brain

Let's talk about this like friends, not doctors.

When you lose someone or something meaningful, your brain doesn't just register sadness — it registers threat. Your nervous system shifts into survival mode. The part of your brain responsible for safety becomes hyper-alert, stress hormones rise, and things like memory, focus, and emotional regulation can start to feel harder to access. This is why grief can leave you feeling foggy, forgetful, on edge, exhausted, emotionally sensitive, detached, or overwhelmed.

Your brain is trying to make sense of a world that suddenly feels different.

And here's something important: the brain stores emotional attachments deeply. So when someone or something disappears from your daily life, your system keeps expecting them to be there. That's why you might reach for your phone without thinking. That's why certain places hurt. That's why anniversaries sting.

Your nervous system is adjusting to absence.

Not weakness.

Adjustment.

In psychology, this is understood as attachment disruption — your system learning how to live without something that once felt essential to your sense of safety. And that kind of adjustment takes time, patience, and a lot of compassion for yourself.

Grief Lives in the Body Too

Grief doesn't move in straight lines, and it isn't something you wake up one day having fully healed from. It also isn't only emotional — it lives in the body. You may notice tightness in your chest, a lump in your throat, stomach discomfort, changes in appetite, disrupted sleep, aches and pains, or a level of fatigue that feels unfamiliar.

There's a biological reason for this. When you experience loss, your body releases stress hormones that affect digestion, muscles, immune function, and sleep cycles. In simple terms, your body is responding to what your heart has been carrying.

So if you've been telling yourself to push through physical exhaustion or strange symptoms, I want to gently invite you to pause. Your body has been working hard to hold everything you've been through.

That deserves compassion.

You don't need to fight your body.

You can begin by listening to it.

The Emotional Cycles of Grief

Grief doesn't move in straight lines. You don't wake up one day and suddenly feel healed. Instead, emotions come in cycles. Some days you feel okay. Some days you don't. Some moments feel peaceful, and others feel heavy. You may move through sadness, anger, guilt, relief, longing, fear, hope, and even joy — sometimes all in the same day.

If that feels overwhelming, I want you to know this doesn't mean you're unstable.

It means your nervous system is processing change.

These emotional shifts are part of adaptation after loss. Your system is learning how to live in a world that feels different now. Grief moves in waves, and waves don't follow schedules.

They rise. They fall. And slowly, over time, you learn how to ride them with more gentleness toward yourself.

Carrying Loss While Still Building Life

Here's a truth that often goes unspoken: you don't have to wait until grief is gone to live again. You don't have to be completely healed to move forward. And you don't have to forget what you lost in order to build something new.

You carry loss with you. And you also carry possibility.

Both can exist at the same time.

You can miss someone deeply and still laugh. You can feel broken and still show up. You can grieve and still dream. In psychology, this is called emotional coexistence — the ability to hold pain and hope together. It isn't betrayal. It's resilience. It's adaptation. It's your nervous system learning how to hold both sorrow and life at once.

Thriving after loss doesn't mean replacing what was taken from you. It means learning how to live alongside it — allowing your heart to expand around what you carry, instead of closing because of it.

And that quiet expansion is where healing begins.

You Are Not Behind in Your Healing

If you've been judging yourself for still crying, still feeling numb, still feeling angry, still missing them, or still struggling, I want you to pause for a moment and hear this gently.

There is no schedule for grief. There is no "right" speed. And there is no prize for healing faster.

You are not behind.

You are processing something real.

Healing isn't measured by how quickly pain disappears. It's about learning how to carry what happened with less suffering over time. That kind of integration doesn't happen overnight. It unfolds slowly, in layers, in moments you don't always notice.

And that's okay.

You're allowed to take the time your heart needs.

I want you to take some time to reflect on your life right now.

Ask yourself gently:

Where am I judging myself right now?

Write whatever comes up.

Then ask:

What would I say to a friend in this same place?

Offer that same kindness to yourself.

Let's complete this quick but gentle practice.

Take a slow breath.

Place one hand on your chest.

Say quietly:
I am not broken.
I am grieving.
And I am allowed to take my time.

Come back to this practice anytime you feel you need or want to.

PART TWO: UNDERSTANDING YOUR EXPERIENCE

Chapter 4

Grief Is Not Linear

"Healing doesn't move in straight lines. It moves in waves — and every wave is part of becoming."

If you've ever had a good day followed by a hard one and found yourself thinking, I was doing better… why do I feel like I'm going backward? I want you to know you're not alone — and you're not broken.

Grief doesn't move in straight lines. It doesn't follow calendars or respect milestones. It doesn't care how much progress you think you've made. Instead, it moves in waves. Some days feel lighter. Some days feel heavy. Some moments feel peaceful. Others feel overwhelming. And sometimes those shifts happen within the same hour.

This is the natural rhythm of emotional processing after loss. Your nervous system is finding its way through something that changed your world. These fluctuations aren't failure.

This is how grief works.

And each wave, even the hard ones, is part of your healing.

The Truth About "Stages"

You may have heard about the stages of grief, often described as a series of steps — denial, anger, bargaining, sadness, and acceptance. It can sound like you're supposed to move neatly from one emotion to the next and eventually arrive at some final destination called healed. But real grief doesn't work that way.

Instead, you might feel acceptance one day and anger the next. You may experience peace in the morning and sadness in the evening. You might think you've processed something, only to find it rising again weeks later. When that happens, it can feel confusing, like you're going backward. But you aren't.

It means grief is layered.

In psychology, we understand these "stages" not as steps, but as experiences. They come and go. They overlap. They repeat. And they show up in different orders for different people. There is no correct sequence. There's no timeline to follow.

There is only your process.

And whatever your grief looks like, it belongs.

Why Emotions Circle Back

Let's talk about this gently and simply. When you experience loss, your brain stores emotional memories right alongside ordinary ones. That means certain sights, sounds, smells, dates, or places can suddenly bring feelings back to the surface — even when you weren't consciously thinking about your loss. In psychology, this is called *emotional recall*. Your nervous system remembers.

That's why a song can make your chest tighten. That's why walking into a familiar place can bring tears. That's why random moments can suddenly feel heavy for no obvious reason.

Your brain is reconnecting with stored emotion.

Not sabotaging your healing.

Supporting it.

Grief isn't something your mind processes once and then moves on from. It's something your nervous system revisits as it slowly learns how to live in a world that has changed. Each return is part of that adaptation. And while it can feel unsettling, it's actually a sign that your system is integrating what happened — gently, in its own time.

Living Between Two Worlds

There's something many grieving people experience that doesn't get talked about enough.

It can feel like you're living in two realities at once.

In one reality, you know what happened. You know they're gone. You understand it logically. You're learning how to move through your days without them.

And in the other reality, your body hasn't caught up yet.

Your nervous system still expects the text.
Still listens for the door.
Still reaches for your phone.
Still waits for them to come home.

You might find yourself thinking, *I know they're not coming…* while simultaneously feeling like they might walk in any moment.

This can be deeply disorienting. You may wonder if something is wrong with you.

There isn't.

This is how attachment works.

Your logical brain understands loss faster than your nervous system does. Emotional bonds live in the body, not just the mind. So even when you consciously know someone is gone, your system continues to search for them. It keeps expecting familiar patterns. Familiar routines. Familiar presence.

Psychology calls this attachment persistence.

I call it love trying to find its way in a world that suddenly changed.

This is why you might reach for your phone without realizing it. Why certain times of day feel heavier. Why quiet moments feel loud. Why your heart still waits for things your mind already knows won't happen.

You're not relapsing.

You're integrating.

For me, this showed up in very real, physical ways. My mind and emotions would drift back into the life I had before the loss, even though my body was living in the life after. I needed something tangible to help me stay grounded in the present. That's why I chose tattoos — not for decoration, but as anchors. Gentle reminders on my skin that this is my current reality. That I'm here. That I survived. That this chapter is real.

They became markers of the life I'm living now, helping me orient myself when grief pulled me backward.

You may not use tattoos. You might use photos, objects, routines, or grounding practices. But the instinct is the same. Your body is learning a new world. And learning takes time.

This space between knowing and feeling can be painful. It can make grief feel confusing and unpredictable. But it's part of healing. Each time your nervous system notices absence, each time you gently return to the present, your body slowly updates its understanding of safety, reality, and connection.

You are not broken for still expecting them.

You are human.

You loved deeply.

And your system is doing its best to adapt to something that was never supposed to happen.

Triggers and Anniversaries

Triggers don't always announce themselves. Sometimes they're obvious — birthdays, holidays, anniversaries. Other times they're quiet — a smell, a laugh, a familiar routine, or a memory that slips in without warning. And sometimes they seem to come out of nowhere. You can be driving, folding laundry, or standing in line at the store when suddenly the weight returns.

When that happens, it doesn't mean you haven't healed.

It means your body remembers.

In psychology, this is called implicit memory — the way your nervous system holds experiences even when your mind isn't actively thinking about them. Anniversaries can be especially powerful because your nervous system tracks time. Even if you don't consciously notice the date, your body often does. That's why certain days, weeks or months may feel heavier, and why emotions can surface without a clear reason.

There is a reason.

Your system is honoring what mattered.

And that remembering, as tender as it can be, is part of how love continues to live inside you.

Sudden Waves of Grief

You may catch yourself thinking, *I thought I was okay… why am I crying again? Why does this still hurt?* When those questions come up, it can feel confusing or discouraging. But grief arrives in waves because your capacity to feel it also comes in waves. Sometimes your nervous system has space to process what you're carrying. Sometimes it needs rest. And sometimes it protects you by giving you breaks.

This is why grief can feel unpredictable.

It rises.
It falls.
It pauses.
It returns.

This is the body's natural rhythm of processing loss. Each wave is your system learning something new about survival, meaning, and adaptation. It isn't random, and it isn't failure.

You are not going backward.

You are integrating loss.

And that integration is happening quietly, gently, in ways you don't always see — but it is happening.

Why Good Days Followed by Bad Days Are Normal

A good day doesn't erase your grief. And a hard day doesn't undo your healing. Both belong in the same journey. You can have moments of joy and still deeply miss what you lost. You can laugh and cry in the same afternoon. You can feel grateful and heartbroken at once.

That doesn't make you confused.

It makes you human.

In psychology, this is called emotional coexistence — the ability to hold multiple truths at the same time. Healing isn't about reaching a place where pain disappears. It's about gently expanding your capacity to carry both sorrow and joy in the same heart.

And over time, that capacity grows.

Not because the loss fades — but because you do.

Permission to Feel Inconsistent

If you've been judging yourself for feeling emotionally inconsistent, I want to invite you to pause for a moment. You're allowed to have days where you feel strong, and days where you feel fragile. You're allowed to feel hopeful one moment and exhausted the next. That back-and-forth doesn't mean you're doing grief wrong.

There is no emotional standard you have to meet.

There is no timeline you're supposed to follow.

And there is no version of grief you're required to perform.

Emotional fluctuation after loss is completely normal — your nervous system is finding its way through something that changed your world. You don't have to steady yourself before you're ready.

You are allowed to be exactly where you are.

And that, right now, is enough.

Remember,

There may be moments when you feel like you've made real progress, only to be surprised by another wave of grief. When that happens, it can feel discouraging — like you've somehow gone backward. But that isn't what's happening. You haven't lost ground. You're healing in layers.

Grief doesn't move forward in a straight line. It moves more like a spiral. Each time something resurfaces, you meet it with a little more awareness, a little more strength, and a little more experience than before — even when it doesn't feel that way in the moment.

This is part of the healing process. Your system revisits emotions and memories as it becomes safe enough to process them. It's not regression. It's progress unfolding slowly.

You are not starting over.

You are continuing — gently, bravely, and in your own time.

I want you to take some time to reflect on your life right now.

Ask yourself:

What tends to trigger waves of grief for me?
Dates?
Places?
Memories?
Unexpected moments?

Write whatever comes up.

Awareness brings gentleness.

Let's complete this quick but gentle practice.

Take a slow breath.

Place one hand on your chest.

Say quietly:

I am not going backward.
I am healing in layers.
I am allowed to feel what I feel.

Come back to this practice anytime you feel you need or want to.

Chapter 5

Survival Mode

"You are not lazy. You are surviving something that asked more of you than most people can see."

If you've been feeling stuck, numb, exhausted, or disconnected, this part is for you. Not because something is wrong with you — but because there's a good chance you've been surviving.

Most people don't realize when they've slipped into survival mode. They tell themselves they're lazy, unmotivated, burned out, or broken. But survival mode isn't a personality flaw. It's a nervous system response. It's what happens when your body and mind have been under prolonged stress or loss.

And grief is one of the strongest triggers for it.

Survival mode is understood as your system shifting into protection when life feels overwhelming. Your body prioritizes getting through the day over feeling connected, motivated, or hopeful. Seeing this through a compassionate lens can change everything. You're not failing.

You've been adapting.

And recognizing that is the first gentle step toward healing.

What Survival Mode Looks Like

Survival mode doesn't always look dramatic. Sometimes it's quiet. It shows up as going through the motions, feeling emotionally flat, struggling to get out of bed, forgetting things easily, or moving through life on autopilot. It can look like overworking to avoid feeling, staying busy so you don't have to sit with your thoughts, feeling disconnected from your body, avoiding emotions, or feeling numb instead of sad.

You may still show up. You may still function. You may still take care of everyone else.

But inside, you feel tired in a way sleep doesn't fix.

In psychology, this is often described as emotional exhaustion or nervous system depletion. Your body has been carrying prolonged stress, quietly doing everything it can to keep you moving forward. This isn't weakness.

This is survival.

And recognizing it with compassion is the beginning of something softer.

How Survival Mode Affects Your Body

When your nervous system feels overwhelmed, it naturally shifts into protection. Your body begins to prioritize safety over creativity, connection, or joy. You might notice constant fatigue, muscle tension, digestive issues, headaches, poor sleep, lowered immunity, or a heavy feeling in your chest. These sensations can feel confusing or frustrating, especially when you don't recognize yourself physically anymore.

But this isn't your body failing you.

It's conserving energy. It's staying alert. It's doing what it knows how to do to keep you going.

Not thriving.

Just surviving.

In psychology, this is understood as prolonged stress activation — your system remaining on high alert after loss. Seeing it this way allows you to meet your body with compassion instead of criticism.

Your body has been carrying more than you realize.

And when it feels safe enough, it will slowly begin to soften again.

How It Affects Your Thoughts

Survival mode also changes how you think. You may notice brain fog, difficulty concentrating, racing thoughts, harsh self-talk, getting stuck in mental loops, or struggling to make decisions. When your nervous system is focused on immediate safety, it doesn't have much space left for long-term vision. So dreaming feels hard. Planning feels overwhelming. Everything starts to feel heavier.

That isn't because you've lost your ability.

It's because your system is overloaded.

This is a natural response to prolonged stress. Your brain has shifted into protection mode, prioritizing survival over creativity or clarity. Understanding this can soften frustration with yourself. Your mind hasn't failed you — it's been working overtime to keep you going.

And with gentleness and time, that mental space can slowly begin to open again.

How It Shows Up in Your Habits

Survival mode often shows up in the small details of everyday life. You may notice yourself overworking, scrolling mindlessly, avoiding people, canceling plans, neglecting self-care, eating differently, or sleeping too much or too little. None of these are personal failures.

They're coping strategies.

These kinds of shifts are your nervous system trying to regulate itself after stress or loss. Your body is searching for ways to manage overwhelm, conserve energy, or find distraction when things feel heavy. Seeing these patterns through this lens can help replace judgment with compassion.

You haven't been doing life wrong.

You've been adapting.

And recognizing that is part of learning how to care for yourself more gently.

The Freeze Response

One common response to trauma and grief is something called *freeze*. This is when you feel stuck — paralyzed, unable to move forward, even though you want change and relief. You may know what you'd like to do, but your body doesn't seem to cooperate. If that's been your experience, I want you to hear this clearly: this isn't laziness.

It's your nervous system trying to protect you from overwhelm.

In psychology, freeze happens when fight or flight feels impossible, so your body chooses stillness instead. It's a survival strategy, not a personal failure. Your system is conserving energy, waiting for safety.

Understanding this can soften self-blame. You're not broken — you're responding to something that felt too much. And with time, gentleness, and support, movement can begin again, one small step at a time.

Autopilot Living

Many people find themselves living in survival mode without even realizing it. They wake up, do what needs to be done, go to bed, and repeat. Days begin to feel mechanical. Joy feels distant. Connection feels harder to reach. You may even feel like you're watching your life instead of truly living it.

In psychology, this is often described as *autopilot* — a state your nervous system slips into after loss or prolonged stress. It's a way of conserving energy when everything feels heavy. Your body keeps you moving forward, even when your heart hasn't caught up yet.

If this feels familiar, you're not broken.

You're adapting.

And awareness is the first gentle step toward coming back into your life, one moment at a time.

Hyper-Independence

Another way survival mode can show up is through hyper-independence. You may notice yourself stopping asking for help, carrying everything on your own, and telling yourself that you've got this, that you don't need anyone, that it's easier to handle things by yourself. On the surface, it can look like strength. But underneath, it's often a protective response that develops after grief or trauma — a way of guarding your heart from further disappointment.

In psychology, this is understood as a self-reliance survival strategy. Your nervous system learns that depending on others feels risky, so it chooses control instead. While this can help you get through hard moments, it can also quietly increase isolation over time.

You don't have to shame yourself for this.

It simply means you've been doing your best to stay safe.

And when you're ready, even allowing one small connection back in can begin to soften that loneliness.

Emotional Shutdown and Dissociation

Sometimes survival mode shows up as emotional shutdown. You might feel disconnected, flat, numb, or even like you're watching your life from outside your body. In psychology, this is called dissociation — and it's your nervous system's way of giving you a break from overwhelming emotion.

It doesn't mean you don't care.

It doesn't mean you've stopped loving.

It simply means your body is doing what it knows how to do to help you cope.

This kind of response often appears when feelings feel too big to hold all at once. And when you understand it through this lens, it becomes easier to meet yourself with compassion instead of fear. Your system hasn't failed you.

It's been protecting you.

Overworking as Avoidance

Some people survive by staying busy. They work, clean, organize, and distract themselves because slowing down would mean feeling — and feeling doesn't always feel safe. So they stay in motion. They fill every quiet moment. They keep their hands moving and their minds occupied.

In psychology, this is understood as a form of avoidance — not laziness or denial, but a nervous system strategy to prevent emotional overwhelm. It's another way your body tries to protect you.

This, too, is survival.

And recognizing it with compassion, rather than judgment, is part of learning how to care for yourself in gentler ways.

Survival vs Thriving: A Gentle Self-Check

Take a moment with this. There are no wrong answers here — just awareness.

Survival mode often shows up as constant exhaustion, feeling numb or disconnected, moving through your days on autopilot, avoiding emotions, overworking, struggling to focus, feeling stuck, or carrying everything on your own. Thriving, on the other hand, begins to look quieter and softer. It shows up as small moments of peace, growing emotional awareness, asking for support, resting without guilt, noticing tiny sparks of hope, or feeling present every once in a while.

If you recognize yourself more in survival than in thriving, pause.

This isn't a judgment.

This is information.

Noticing where you are is the first step toward change. Awareness helps your nervous system understand its current state, and that understanding creates space for something new to emerge. You don't need to push yourself forward right now. You don't need to fix anything.

Simply seeing yourself with honesty and compassion is already part of your healing.

You Are Not Lazy. You Are Surviving.

Let this settle into you for a moment.

You are not lazy. You are not broken. And you are not failing at life. You have been carrying loss, and your nervous system has been doing its best to protect you. What you may be experiencing is survival mode — the natural response that happens when you've had to be strong for too long.

Recognizing this is powerful. Awareness is often the first doorway to healing. You can't soften what you don't yet see. And this isn't about forcing change or fixing yourself.

It's about noticing.

Noticing where you are.
Noticing what you've been carrying.
Noticing what your body has been doing to keep you going.

That quiet awareness is where healing begins.

I want you to take some time to reflect on your life right now.

Ask yourself:

Where do I see survival mode in my life right now?

Write whatever comes up.

Be honest.

Be gentle.

Let's complete this quick but gentle practice.

Place one hand on your chest.

Take a slow breath.

Say quietly:
I am not lazy.
I am surviving.
And awareness is the beginning of healing.

Come back to this practice anytime you feel you need or want to.

PART THREE: FROM SURVIVING TO LIVING AGAIN

Chapter 6

Permission to Feel Everything

"You don't have to fix your feelings. You just have to let them be heard."

If you've been holding yourself together for a long time, this part may feel especially tender. And that's okay. Grief doesn't live only in memories — it lives in the body. When emotions aren't given space to move, they don't disappear. They stay stored inside us.

Many people survive loss by becoming emotionally efficient. They compartmentalize. They stay busy. They push feelings aside so they can keep functioning. They tell themselves they'll deal with it later, that they can't fall apart right now, that they have to be strong. And sometimes, in the middle of crisis, that strength is necessary.

But eventually, what you don't feel still asks to be felt.

This part of your healing isn't about breaking down. It's about allowing. It's about giving your body permission to soften, even just a little. In psychology, this is the beginning of emotional release — creating safety for what's been held to finally have a voice.

You don't have to rush it.

You don't have to force anything.

You're simply being invited to let yourself feel, in whatever way feels possible right now.

You Are Allowed to Feel All of It

Grief brings so much more than sadness. It can carry anger, guilt, relief, joy, and confusion — sometimes all at once. You may feel angry about what happened, angry at people who didn't show up, or even angry at life itself. You might find yourself replaying things you said or didn't say, feeling guilt for surviving, or guilt for laughing again. If your loss followed a long illness or struggle, you may even feel relief — and then feel guilty for feeling that too. You might catch moments of joy and immediately wonder if that somehow makes you disloyal to what you lost. And underneath it all, you may feel confused about who you are now.

If any of this sounds familiar, I want you to know something important: all of it belongs.

None of these feelings make you a bad person. They're human responses to loss. In psychology, this is called emotional complexity — the ability to hold multiple, even contradictory emotions at the same time. It's not a flaw. It's part of being alive after something meaningful has been taken away.

You don't need to edit your emotions. You don't need to make them make sense. And you don't need to justify them.

You are allowed to feel everything.

Emotional Suppression: When Feelings Get Stuck

Many of us learned early on how to suppress our emotions. Maybe you were told not to cry. Maybe you had to grow up fast. Maybe there simply wasn't space for your feelings, so you learned to swallow them and keep going. That kind of adaptation makes sense when you're trying to survive.

But emotions don't disappear when they're ignored.

They settle into the body.

In psychology and trauma research, this is well understood. Unexpressed feelings often show up physically — as tension, fatigue, headaches, tightness in the chest, stomach issues, restlessness, or numbness. Your body carries what your voice never had the chance to say.

This isn't weakness.

It's biology.

Feelings are meant to move. And when they're finally given permission, even gently, your system begins to soften in ways that words alone can't reach.

Letting Feelings Move Through the Body

Emotions are energy. They're meant to move, not stay trapped inside you. And you don't have to relive everything in order to release it. Often, what your body needs most is presence. That might look like taking a few slow breaths and noticing where you feel heaviness, placing a hand on your heart or belly, letting tears come if they come, gently shaking out your arms or legs, stretching, writing without censoring yourself, or simply sitting quietly and naming what you feel.

None of this has to be dramatic.

In psychology, even small moments of emotional permission help regulate the nervous system. Letting yourself feel for even a minute or two tells your body that it's safe to soften. You don't need a big breakthrough. You don't need to force anything. These quiet acts of attention matter. They teach your system that you're listening — and that, over time, creates space for healing.

Emotional Release Is Not Losing Control

Many people avoid feeling because they're afraid they won't be able to stop once they start. That fear makes sense, especially when emotions feel overwhelming. But feelings don't come to destroy you. They come to be witnessed. You don't have to drown in them. You can let them move through you, like waves — they rise, they peak, and they soften.

In psychology, this is called emotional processing. Each time you allow an emotion to be felt safely, your body learns something important: *I can survive this.* That awareness builds emotional resilience over time. It teaches your nervous system that feelings are temporary, not dangerous.

You don't lose control by allowing emotion.

You regain trust in yourself.

And that trust becomes part of your healing.

You Don't Have to Be Strong Here

This book is meant to be a safe place for you. You don't have to perform strength here. You don't have to find the right words, and you don't have to pretend you're okay. You only need to be honest with yourself. Whatever you're feeling right now is welcome.

There's no pressure to hold it together on these pages. You're allowed to soften. You're allowed to feel. And you're allowed to take this moment exactly as it comes.

I want you to take some time to reflect on your life right now.

Ask yourself gently:

What emotion have I been holding in the most?
Anger?
Sadness?
Guilt?
Fear?
Numbness?

Write it down. Then ask:

What does my body need right now?
Rest?
Movement?
Quiet?
Comfort?

Let the answer guide you.

Let's complete this quick but gentle practice.

Close your eyes for a moment.

Take a slow breath.

Place one hand on your chest.

Say quietly:
I am allowed to feel.
My emotions are safe here.
I don't have to rush my healing.

Come back to this practice anytime you feel you need or want to.

Chapter 7

Choosing to Live Again

"Living again doesn't erase what you lost. It honors it by allowing your heart to keep beating."

There often comes a quiet moment in grief when something inside you gently asks, Okay… now what? Not loudly. Not dramatically. Just a soft question that rises after you've felt what you've been holding and acknowledged what hurts. Even if you don't feel ready, life is still here, waiting patiently.

This part of your journey isn't about big transformations or sudden clarity. It's about small beginnings. It's about allowing yourself to breathe again. In psychology, this is the beginning of re-engagement — the moment your system starts opening just enough to imagine what might come next.

You don't have to have answers.

You don't have to know the whole path.

You only have to take one gentle step back toward yourself.

You Don't Have to Feel Ready

Many people wait to feel "better" before they allow themselves to move forward. They hope motivation will arrive first, that one day they'll wake up ready. But readiness rarely comes that way. More often, it follows action — not big, dramatic action, but gentle, human steps.

You don't suddenly become full of energy or clarity. You begin with one small choice. You drink a glass of water. You step outside for a moment. You open a window. You make your bed. You send a text. These things may seem insignificant, but they aren't. In psychology, these tiny acts are called *behavioral activation* — small movements that help signal safety and possibility to the nervous system.

They're signs of life quietly re-entering your body.

Momentum doesn't arrive loudly.

It begins softly, through simple moments of care.

And you're allowed to start exactly where you are.

Finding Your Way Back to the Present

Sometimes grief pulls us backward. Not intentionally, and not dramatically — just quietly. A smell, a memory, a familiar time of day, and suddenly your body is somewhere else, back in the life before. If this happens to you, it doesn't mean you're stuck. It means your nervous system is still learning where *now* is. After loss, your body continues to reach for what once felt familiar and safe, even when your mind knows things have changed.

For some of us, it helps to have anchors. Not rules. Not rituals we force. Just gentle reminders that bring us back into our bodies and into the present moment. Anchors can look like many things. For me, they became tattoos — not for appearance, but for grounding. They were quiet markers on my skin that helped me recognize which life I was living now, soft signals to my nervous system that I survived something profound, and that this moment is real.

For you, anchors might be something different. It might be a piece of jewelry, a photo you carry, a morning routine, a scent that feels safe, a song that brings you back, a walk you take every day, a journal you return to, or a place where you pause and breathe. There is no right way.

Anchors don't erase grief. They help your body orient. They gently remind you: *I am here. This is today. I am safe enough right now.*

Over time, these small moments of grounding teach your nervous system something important — that even though life has changed, you are still here inside it. That you can feel pain and presence at the same time. That you don't have to disappear into memory to honor love.

You can stay.

And slowly, your body begins to learn that this world — even changed — is still one you belong in.

Learning to Want More Again

After loss, it's very common for desire to go quiet. You may stop imagining the future, stop making plans, or notice that wanting anything at all feels distant. This doesn't mean your dreams are gone. It means your nervous system has been protecting you from more disappointment. When something meaningful has been taken away, wanting again can feel risky. It can feel disloyal. It can feel scary.

But desire is part of being alive.

In psychology, this is understood as a protective shutdown — your system temporarily closing off hope to avoid further hurt. And when you're ready, wanting doesn't have to come back all at once. You don't have to reach for everything you used to dream about. You can begin with one small want. More peace. More rest. More connection. More ease.

Let that be enough for now.

Those quiet desires are your body remembering that life still lives inside you — and honoring them, even gently, is part of choosing yourself again.

Releasing Guilt Around Joy

When moments of joy begin to return, many people find themselves carrying guilt alongside them. You might catch yourself wondering how you can laugh when you've lost so much, or questioning whether it's okay to enjoy a moment, or worrying about what others might think. Those thoughts are common, especially when grief is still close to the surface.

But joy doesn't erase love. It doesn't minimize loss. And it doesn't betray what mattered.

Joy is simply evidence that your heart is still capable of holding life.

In psychology, this is understood as emotional integration — the ability to carry both sorrow and happiness at the same time. One doesn't cancel the other. They coexist. You can miss deeply and still smile. You can grieve and still feel warmth. Both can live in the same body, in the same moment.

You are allowed to experience happiness again.

Even while grieving.

And sometimes, especially while grieving.

Allowing Desire After Loss

Grief has a way of shrinking your world. For a while, everything becomes about surviving. You focus on getting through the day, and dreaming quietly fades into the background. But thriving begins when you allow yourself to expand again — not through pressure, but through permission.

It starts with listening inward and asking what would feel supportive right now. Not what sounds impressive. Not what looks productive. Just what feels kind to your nervous system in this moment. Maybe it's more sleep. Maybe it's gentle movement. Maybe it's sitting in silence. Maybe it's trying something new, even in a small way.

Desire doesn't have to be big.

It just has to be honest.

This is part of re-engaging with life after loss — allowing yourself to notice what brings even a quiet sense of comfort or curiosity. These small signals of desire are your system remembering that there is still life available to you. And honoring them, little by little, helps your world begin to open again.

Small Choices Create Big Healing

Healing doesn't happen through grand gestures or dramatic turning points. It grows quietly, through tiny, repeated acts of care. One walk. One deep breath. One nourishing meal. One honest conversation. One moment of rest. Each small choice sends a message to your nervous system that you are safe enough to keep going.

That's how momentum builds.

Not through force.

Through consistency.

These small, steady actions are what help the body and mind reestablish a sense of stability after loss. They may feel insignificant in the moment, but over time they create a foundation of safety and trust within yourself. And that foundation is what allows healing to take root.

You don't have to do everything.

You just have to keep choosing yourself, one gentle moment at a time.

Re-Engaging With Life

Choosing to live again doesn't mean forgetting what you lost. It means allowing space for what still exists. It's the quiet decision to show up to your own life, even when everything feels tender. It's letting color slowly return, in small and unexpected ways.

You don't have to leap forward.

You can take one step.

You don't have to run.

You're allowed to pause.

And you don't have to feel brave.

You just have to be willing.

In psychology, healing is understood as a gradual re-engagement with life — not a sudden transformation. Your nervous system needs time to feel safe enough to open back up. Every gentle moment of presence, every small choice to participate again, tells your body that it's okay to keep living.

And that, in itself, is courage.

You Are Allowed to Move Forward

Let this settle into your heart for a moment.

You are allowed to live fully again. You are allowed to dream again. You are allowed to experience abundance again. Moving forward doesn't mean leaving your loved one behind — it means carrying them with you in a new way. Their love, their influence, the memories you hold… all of that becomes part of who you are becoming.

In psychology, this is called *continuing bonds* — the understanding that healthy healing doesn't require forgetting. It allows space for both remembrance and renewal. You don't have to choose between honoring what was and embracing what's ahead.

Both can exist together.

And when you're ready — in your own time — you're allowed to let life expand again.

I want you to take some time to reflect on your life right now.

Ask yourself:

What is one small thing I can do today that supports my healing?

Write it down.

Then do it gently.

Let's complete this quick but gentle practice.

Take a slow breath.

Place one hand on your chest.

Say quietly:

> *I am allowed to live again.*
> *I am allowed to feel hope.*
> *One small step is enough.*

Come back to this practice anytime you feel you need or want to.

PART FOUR: YOUR SUPPORT SYSTEM MATTERS

Chapter 8

You Don't Have to Do This Alone

"You were never meant to carry grief by yourself."

Grief has a quiet way of convincing you that you have to carry everything by yourself. You may start to feel like no one truly understands, or worry that reaching out would make you a burden. Sometimes it feels safer to keep everything inside. You might tell yourself you'll handle it on your own, that other people have their own problems, that it's easier not to ask for anything.

And if those thoughts sound familiar, you're not weak — you're protecting yourself.

But here's something important your grief may be trying to hide from you: humans were never meant to grieve in isolation. From a psychological standpoint, connection is one of the primary ways our nervous systems heal. We regulate through relationships. We soften when we're seen. Even small moments of shared presence can ease the weight you're carrying.

You don't have to walk this alone.

You're allowed to need support.

And you deserve to be supported — in whatever gentle ways feel possible right now.

What a Support System Really Is

When people hear the phrase support system, they often imagine a perfect circle of emotionally available people who always know what to say and never disappear. But that's rarely how real life works.

Your support system doesn't have to be big. It doesn't have to be ideal. And it doesn't have to look the way you thought it would.

Support can come from many places — family, friends, therapists, doctors, spiritual leaders, support groups, online communities, coworkers, neighbors, and sometimes even your pets. In psychology, support is defined less by who someone is to you and more by how they help your nervous system feel less alone.

Sometimes support looks like a conversation. Sometimes it's a text message. Sometimes it's sitting quietly with someone who doesn't try to fix anything. Sometimes it's professional care. And sometimes it's your pet staying close while you cry.

Support is anyone or anything that reminds you you're not carrying this by yourself.

It doesn't have to be perfect.

It just has to exist.

Why Asking for Help Feels Hard

Many people struggle to reach out after loss, and there are so many understandable reasons why. You may worry about seeming weak. You might be afraid of becoming a burden. Maybe you've been disappointed before. Maybe you're used to being the strong one. Or maybe you simply don't know what to say.

If any of that feels familiar, there is nothing wrong with you.

You're protecting yourself.

In psychology, this is a natural response to vulnerability — especially after you've already been hurt. Your nervous system is trying to keep you safe from further disappointment. And that makes sense. But healing often asks for something gentle and brave at the same time: allowing someone to see you, even just a little.

You don't have to share everything.

You don't have to have it all figured out.

Sometimes letting one safe person witness your truth is enough to soften the weight you've been carrying.

How to Ask for Help (Without Overthinking It)

You don't need a long explanation. You don't need perfect words. You just need honesty.

Reaching out can be as simple as letting someone know and asking:
- "I'm having a hard day. Can we talk for a few minutes?"
- "I don't need advice — I just need someone to listen."
- "Could you check in on me this week?"
- "I'm struggling more than I've been letting on."
- "Can you sit with me for a bit?"

And if asking directly feels like too much, you can start smaller. You might send a heart emoji. Share a memory. Ask how someone else is doing. These gentle gestures still count. In psychology, connection doesn't require grand vulnerability — it begins with small moments of reach. Even tiny signals invite your nervous system back into relationship.

Connection doesn't have to be dramatic.

It just has to begin.

And you're allowed to take that first step in whatever way feels safest right now.

When Your Support System Feels Small

Some people have large families. Some don't. Some are surrounded by close friends. Others have watched relationships shift or fade in the wake of grief. If your support system feels smaller than you hoped right now, that doesn't mean you'll always be alone. It simply means this is where you're starting.

Support can be built.

Sometimes it begins with a therapist or counselor. Sometimes it grows through a grief support group, an online community, a faith-based space, or even local gatherings and volunteer opportunities. And sometimes it starts quietly — with one person who listens, one place that feels safe, one connection that reminds you you're not invisible.

Even one safe person makes a difference.

And if, in this moment, this book feels like that safe place, that counts too.

You're allowed to begin exactly where you are.

Setting Boundaries Is Part of Support

Not everyone will show up in the ways you need. Some people avoid grief altogether. Some minimize it. Some rush to fix it. And some quietly disappear. All of that can hurt more than you expect.

But their response doesn't mean your grief is too much.

It simply means they're meeting your pain with the limits of their own emotional capacity.

You're allowed to protect your energy in this season. You're allowed to pause conversations that feel overwhelming. You're allowed to name when something doesn't feel supportive. Saying you're not ready to talk, that you need space, or that a comment wasn't helpful isn't rude — it's honest.

In psychology, boundaries are understood as a form of self-regulation. They help your nervous system stay balanced. They allow you to remain open without becoming depleted.

Support doesn't mean letting everything in.

Sometimes, support looks like choosing what — and who — you allow close.

And that, too, is part of healing.

You Deserve Care

You were never meant to carry everything alone. Healing isn't a solo journey, even when it feels that way sometimes. You deserve connection. You deserve compassion. You deserve to be supported as you find your way forward.

And if reaching out feels hard, I want you to know this: it isn't weakness. It's courage. It's your nervous system asking for safety. It's your heart remembering that humans heal in relationship. Allowing yourself to be seen — even by one safe person — is an act of strength.

You don't have to do this perfectly.

You just have to let yourself be held, in whatever small ways feel possible right now.

I want you to take some time to reflect on your life right now.

Ask yourself:

Who feels safest to reach out to right now?

It doesn't have to be perfect. Just honest.

Write their name. Then ask:

What kind of support do I need today?
Listening?
Company?
Rest?
Professional help?

Let yourself receive.

Let's complete this quick but gentle practice.

Take a slow breath.

Place one hand on your chest.

Say quietly:
I don't have to do this alone.
Support is allowed.
Connection is part of healing.

Come back to this practice anytime you feel you need or want to.

Chapter 9

When People Don't Show Up the Way You Expected

"Not everyone can meet you in grief — and that hurts. But you still deserve safe connection."

One of the quiet heartbreaks of grief is realizing that some people won't show up the way you thought they would. You may have assumed certain friends would check in. You may have believed family would be more present. You may have pictured support looking a very specific way. And when it doesn't — when the calls don't come, when the silence stretches, when presence feels uneven — it hurts. Sometimes deeply.

Grief doesn't just reveal loss.

It reveals relationships.

It shows you who has the capacity to stay close in hard moments, and who doesn't know how to hold pain. That realization can feel almost as heavy as the original loss. And if you find yourself grieving both what happened and who didn't show up, that makes sense. Both deserve space. Both matter.

You're not wrong for needing more.

You're not weak for noticing the absence.

You're simply seeing clearly — and clarity, even when painful, is part of healing.

The Secondary Loss No One Talks About

After a major loss, many people experience something they never expected — they lose people too. Not through death, but through distance. Conversations fade. Invitations stop. Messages go unanswered. People change. And suddenly, alongside your primary grief, you find yourself carrying another quiet heartbreak.

This is sometimes called *secondary loss* — the loss of connection, safety, or community that often follows a major life change. And it can feel just as painful.

You may start asking yourself questions that cut deep. Did I do something wrong? Am I too much? Why don't they care?

If those thoughts have crossed your mind, I want to say this gently: most people don't disappear because you are unworthy. They pull away because grief makes them uncomfortable. Your loss reminds them of vulnerability, of impermanence, of things they don't know how to hold.

In psychology, this is understood as emotional avoidance — a protective response when someone feels overwhelmed by another person's pain. It doesn't make it hurt less, but it can help you stop turning their distance inward.

You didn't cause this.

Your grief didn't make you unlovable.

It simply revealed who had the capacity to stay, and who didn't — at least in this season.

And that realization, while painful, is part of learning where safety truly lives.

Why People Pull Away

Many people simply don't know how to sit with pain. Some are afraid of saying the wrong thing. Some can't fully understand grief unless they've lived it themselves. Some feel helpless in the face of loss. Others avoid discomfort altogether. And some assume you're "doing better" simply because you look okay on the outside.

There are also those who pull back because your loss touches their own fears — reminding them how fragile life can be.

None of this excuses the hurt it causes. But it can help explain it.

In psychology, this is often described as avoidance or emotional distancing. When people don't have the tools to hold heavy emotions, they retreat. Not always because they don't care — but because they don't know how to care in a way that feels safe to them.

That doesn't mean your pain is too much.

It means grief exposes emotional limits.

And while that realization can be deeply disappointing, it can also bring clarity. It helps you see who is able to meet you with presence, and who simply isn't — at least right now.

You don't have to make that personal.

Your grief deserves compassion, even when others don't know how to offer it.

Changed Relationships Are Part of Grief

Grief changes you. And when you change, the way you relate to others often changes too. You may notice that some relationships deepen, some begin to feel strained, some quietly fade, and others fall away altogether. That can be incredibly painful, especially when you're already carrying so much.

But this, too, is part of becoming.

Loss reshapes your inner world, and not everyone is meant to walk every season of your life with you. Some people are here for a chapter. Some stay longer. Some are only meant to support you through a moment. That doesn't diminish what they meant — it simply reflects the natural movement of relationships as we grow and change.

In psychology, this is understood as relational reorganization after trauma. Your nervous system starts seeking different kinds of safety, depth, and understanding. You may find yourself craving authenticity over small talk, emotional presence over proximity.

Letting go of expectations — of who should stay, who should understand, who should show up — is part of healing. It doesn't mean you stop caring. It means you begin honoring where you are now.

And that, too, is an act of self-respect.

Grief Isolation

When people disappear after a loss, grief can start to feel even heavier. You may feel invisible, misunderstood, or quietly abandoned. Sometimes that pain leads you to stop reaching out altogether. You might tell yourself it's safer to stay quiet, safer not to need anyone, safer not to hope for understanding.

And that response makes sense. When connection hurts, retreat can feel protective.

But isolation also makes grief heavier.

Even when relationships shift, you still deserve connection. Even when people disappoint you, you still deserve support. Your nervous system heals in safe connection — this is something psychology has shown again and again. We regulate through relationships. We soften through being seen. Healing doesn't happen in total solitude.

You don't need a crowd.

You don't need perfect people.

You just need spaces where you're allowed to be human.
And those spaces still exist, even if they look different than they used to.

Emotional Self-Protection Is Not Bitterness

After loss, it's very common to notice yourself pulling inward. You may share less, trust more cautiously, or stop expecting much from others altogether. This isn't bitterness. It's protection. Your nervous system has learned what it feels like to be deeply hurt, and now it's doing its best to prevent that from happening again.

That response makes sense.

In trauma psychology, this is understood as emotional self-protection — a natural adaptation when safety has been shaken. Your system is trying to keep you from being overwhelmed. And while that instinct is wise, healing also gently invites balance. It's about learning how to protect yourself without closing your heart completely.

You don't have to give everyone access to your inner world.

You don't have to open up to people who don't feel safe.

You only need a few spaces where you can be real. A few people who listen without fixing. A few moments where you don't have to armor up.

That's enough.

Slowly, carefully, connection can begin to feel possible again — on your terms.

Boundary Setting Is Part of Healing

Not everyone deserves access to your emotional energy — and that's okay. After loss, you may begin to feel more protective of your inner world, and that's not selfish. That's awareness. Boundaries might sound like gently saying you're not ready to talk about something, acknowledging when you need space, naming when a comment doesn't feel supportive, or choosing not to engage in a heavy conversation on a hard day.

These moments of honesty aren't punishment. They're clarity.

Boundaries help protect your healing. They teach people how to meet you with respect. And just as importantly, they give *you* permission to care for yourself without guilt. In psychology, boundaries are understood as a form of emotional regulation — a way your nervous system stays balanced by limiting overwhelm. They allow you to remain open without becoming depleted.

You're allowed to choose what feels safe.

You're allowed to take breaks.

And you're allowed to honor your needs as they change.

That, too, is part of healing.

You Don't Have to Chase People Who Can't Meet You Here

One of the hardest lessons grief teaches is that you don't have to beg for presence. You don't have to over-explain your pain, and you don't have to chase people into understanding. Loss has a way of clarifying what feels safe and what doesn't, and over time you may notice that your nervous system naturally gravitates toward the people who can meet you with care.

You deserve relationships that feel steady. You deserve people who make space for your truth without rushing you or minimizing what you carry. You deserve support that doesn't require you to shrink or perform healing.

And while it can hurt to see who steps back, there is also something quietly powerful about letting the ones who show up truly matter — and allowing the rest to fall away with compassion. Not from bitterness. From self-respect. From the understanding that your energy is precious, especially now.

You don't need everyone.

You just need safe connection.

And that is more than enough.

I want you to take some time to reflect on your life right now.

Ask yourself:

Who has shown up for me, even in small ways?

Write their names. They are apart of your support system. Lean on them when needed and return the love when they need it.

Then ask:

Where do I need stronger boundaries right now?

Be honest. This is about your peace.

Let's complete this quick but gentle practice.

Place one hand on your chest.

Take a slow breath.

Say quietly:
I am allowed to protect my heart.
I am allowed to release expectations.
I deserve supportive connections.

Come back to this practice anytime you feel you need or want to.

PART FIVE: THRIVING IN EVERY AREA OF LIFE

Grief doesn't stay contained in just one part of your life.

It touches everything — your thoughts, your emotions, your body, your faith, your finances, your relationships, and even your sense of purpose. That's why healing can't happen in only one place. You don't just grieve emotionally. You grieve mentally, physically, spiritually, financially, and relationally too.

And thriving means gently rebuilding in all of these areas.

Not all at once.
 Not perfectly.
 One area at a time.

These chapters aren't about becoming a new person overnight. They're about slowly coming back to yourself — learning how to live in your body again, how to trust your mind again, how to reconnect with meaning, and how to move forward in ways that feel supportive and real.

There's no rush here.

Healing unfolds in layers.

And every small step you take matters.

Chapter 10

Mental Healing:
Learning How to Think Softly Again

"Your mind isn't broken. It's been protecting you."

Let's talk about your mind for a moment.

Grief doesn't only change how you feel — it also changes how you think. You may notice that your thoughts feel heavier than they used to, that your focus disappears easily, that you replay moments or conversations, or that your inner voice has become harsher. If any of that feels familiar, you're not imagining it.

Your brain has been trying to protect you.

After loss, the mind naturally shifts into survival mode. The part of your brain responsible for detecting threat becomes more active, while the areas involved in concentration, planning, and creativity tend to quiet down. This pattern is well documented in neuroscience research on grief and trauma. In simple terms, your brain is scanning for danger instead of dreaming about the future.

That's why small decisions can feel exhausting. That's why memory may feel foggy. That's why overthinking becomes automatic.

Not because you're broken.

Because your nervous system has been on guard.

Understanding this can soften self-judgment. Your mind isn't failing you — it's adapting to something deeply destabilizing. And with time, safety, and compassion, it can begin to open back up again.

Slowly. Gently. In its own way.

Something important most people don't tell you

After grief, your thoughts don't always make sense — and that's because they're not trying to be logical. They're trying to protect you.

The brain naturally replays memories and scenarios in an attempt to understand what happened. It loops because it's searching for safety and meaning. Researchers call this rumination, and while it can feel exhausting, it's actually your nervous system trying to regain a sense of control after loss.

The problem isn't that these loops exist.

It's when they start to run everything.

Left unchecked, they can turn into mental habits that keep you stuck. Healing begins when you gently notice them — not with forced positivity, but with awareness. That quiet noticing creates space. It gives your nervous system a chance to settle.

You're not broken for thinking this way.

Your system has been trying to help.

And now, slowly, you're learning how to guide it with compassion.

Let me share something personal

After loss, many people notice themselves becoming harder on their own hearts.

You may start criticizing your productivity, judging your emotions, feeling guilty for resting, or comparing your healing to others. This is incredibly common. Grief creates uncertainty, and when the world feels unstable, the mind often tries to regain control wherever it can. It turns inward. It tightens. It looks for something to manage.

But mental healing isn't about controlling your thoughts.

It's about changing your relationship with them.

Psychologically, thoughts are simply mental events — not instructions and not always truth. You don't have to believe every thought that passes through your mind. You don't have to argue with them either. You can simply notice them, let them move through, and return your attention to the present.

That gentle awareness creates space.

And in that space, compassion begins to grow again.

You're not failing at healing.

You're learning how to meet your mind with kindness after it's been trying to protect you.

And that's powerful.

Let's gently practice changing how you talk to yourself

When you notice your thoughts starting to spiral, it can help to gently name what's happening. Simply saying to yourself, *this is grief thinking,* can create a small but meaningful pause. That one sentence opens space between you and the storm of thoughts.

From there, you might offer yourself something grounding, like *I'm doing the best I can right now,* or *this is hard, and I don't have to rush it,* or *I don't need to have everything figured out today.* These aren't affirmations meant to override reality. They're forms of regulation. They help calm your nervous system and remind your body that it's safe enough to slow down.

Psychologically, this kind of compassionate self-talk shifts you out of survival mode and back into the present. You're not trying to erase what you feel — you're letting your system know that you're here with it.

And that quiet reassurance matters more than you might realize.

Here are a few gentle ways to support your mind right now

Not all at once.

Just one small moment at a time.

Grief drains cognitive energy, often in ways you don't immediately notice. Your mind becomes tired more quickly, and too much input can feel overwhelming. Mental healing usually begins with creating a little more spaciousness. That might mean scrolling less, saying no to extra commitments, taking short quiet breaks, or gently simplifying your day. Your brain doesn't need more stimulation right now — it needs room to breathe.

You may also notice your thoughts looping, replaying the same worries or questions over and over. When that happens, try pausing for a slow breath and shifting your attention into your body — maybe feeling your feet on the floor, noticing your breath, or looking around and naming something you can see. Psychologically, this helps interrupt the stress cycle and reminds your nervous system that it doesn't need to stay stuck in that loop.

And be especially gentle with the way you talk to yourself.

After loss, harsh inner dialogue often sneaks in — thoughts like I should be over this or I'm not doing enough. When you notice that, see if you can meet it with honesty instead of criticism. This is taking time, and that's okay. I showed up in the ways I could today. These small shifts may seem simple, but they matter. Over time, they literally reshape neural pathways, teaching your brain a kinder, safer way to respond.

Mental healing doesn't happen through force.

It happens through patience.

Through softness.

Through choosing compassion again and again — even on the hard days.

Take a moment and reflect with me

Grab your journal or just sit quietly with these questions:
- What thoughts repeat most often lately?
- How do I speak to myself when I'm struggling?
- What would I say to someone I love in this same situation?
- What does my mind need more of right now — rest, reassurance, or clarity?

There are no right answers.

Just honesty.

Here are some simple but effective daily practices to calm your mind and rebuild clarity

Choose one or two.

That's enough.

- Take three slow breaths when you wake up
- Write one compassionate sentence to yourself each morning
- Step outside for five minutes without your phone
- End the day by naming one thing you handled
- Place your hand on your chest when thoughts feel heavy

These tiny moments retrain your nervous system.

They tell your brain:
>   I am safe enough to soften.

Let's complete this quick but gentle practice

Close your eyes.

Take a slow breath.

Place one hand on your chest.

Say quietly:
>   *My mind deserves compassion.*
>   *I am healing, even when I can't see it.*
>   *I am allowed to think softly again.*

Come back to this practice anytime you feel you need or want to.

Mental healing doesn't mean you stop remembering. It means you stop letting grief control your inner dialogue. It means learning how to be kind to your own mind. And that is a powerful beginning.

Chapter 11

Emotional Thriving:
Learning How to Feel Safely Again

"Feeling is not weakness. It is how healing begins."

Let's talk about your emotions for a moment.

After grief, feelings can become overwhelming — or they can go completely quiet. Some people feel everything all at once. Some feel nothing at all. Some swing back and forth between the two. And many don't recognize themselves emotionally anymore.

If that sounds familiar, I want you to hear this gently:
There is nothing wrong with you.

Psychologically, your emotional system has been protecting you. When loss feels too big to hold, your nervous system adapts in whatever way helps you survive — either by flooding you with emotion or by numbing things out. Both are natural responses to trauma.

You haven't lost yourself.

Your system has been doing its best to keep you safe.

And with time, care, and compassion, your emotional world can begin to feel more steady again.

Slowly. Tenderly. In your own time.

Here's what's really happening inside

When you experience loss, your nervous system naturally shifts into survival mode.

Your body releases stress hormones, emotional regulation becomes harder, and your tolerance for overwhelm drops. Small things start to feel big. Big things can feel impossible. Research in trauma psychology shows that grief can temporarily disrupt the brain's ability to regulate emotion — especially when loss is sudden, layered, or prolonged.

In simple terms, your emotional brakes aren't working the way they used to.

So feelings may come out stronger than expected. Or they may shut down completely.

This isn't weakness.

It's biology.

Your system has been doing its best to keep you safe after something deeply destabilizing happened. Understanding this can soften self-judgment. You're not broken — your body has been protecting you.

And with time, safety, and compassion, your nervous system can learn how to regulate again.

Slowly. Gently. In its own way.

Emotional thriving starts with safety, not strength

Most people grow up believing that healing means being strong.

But emotional thriving actually begins with feeling safe. Safe to cry. Safe to feel anger. Safe to experience relief. Safe to let joy return. Safe to say, *"I'm not okay."* When your body doesn't feel emotionally safe, it will usually respond in one of two ways — either flooding you with feelings or shutting them down completely. Both are survival responses. Both are ways your nervous system tries to protect you after something overwhelming.

Neither of these states are permanent.

Psychologically, healing happens when safety is restored. When your system learns that it doesn't have to brace anymore, emotions begin to move more naturally. You don't have to force this process. You just have to create space for yourself to be real.

Strength isn't holding everything together.

Strength is allowing yourself to feel.

And that's where emotional thriving truly begins.

Let's talk about the emotions that often show up after loss

Grief doesn't arrive with just sadness.

It often brings anger, guilt, fear, confusion, loneliness — and sometimes even relief or moments of joy. These emotions can show up in combinations that feel confusing or uncomfortable. You might feel angry and miss someone deeply at the same time. You may notice gratitude alongside heartbreak. If there was long suffering involved, you might even feel relief — and then judge yourself for it.

I want you to know this gently: all of this is normal.

Emotions don't cancel each other out. They coexist. Psychologically, the brain is capable of holding multiple emotional states at once, especially after loss. Feeling one thing doesn't erase another. Having mixed emotions doesn't mean you're doing grief wrong — it means you're human.

There is room for all of it.

Let yourself feel what's here without trying to organize it.

Your heart is learning how to hold complexity.

And that's part of healing.

You don't have to fix your feelings

This part matters.

Emotions don't need solutions — they need permission. Most of us were taught to suppress our feelings, analyze them, or push past them as quickly as possible. But emotions are energy in the body. They naturally move when they're allowed, and they tend to get stuck when they're resisted.

Emotional thriving isn't about controlling how you feel. It's about letting feelings pass through without judging them. Psychologically, this is how the nervous system completes emotional cycles — through presence, not pressure. When you stop trying to fix what you feel and simply allow it, something softens. Space opens.

You don't have to manage your emotions perfectly.

You just have to let them be real.

And that honesty is where healing begins.

Let me share something gentle and powerful

When emotions rise, it can be tempting to immediately ask yourself why you're feeling this way. But there's something gentler — and often more helpful — you can try instead.

You might simply shift your attention to your body and notice where the feeling lives. Maybe it shows up as tightness in your chest, heaviness in your stomach, or a lump in your throat. You don't need to analyze it. Just noticing is enough.

Psychologically, this moves you out of mental loops and into physical awareness, which helps calm the nervous system. You're no longer trying to solve the emotion — you're allowing it to be felt. And that presence alone begins release.

No fixing.
No forcing.

Just quiet attention.

Your body knows what to do when it feels heard.

And every time you offer that kind of listening, you create a little more space inside yourself.

Here are some simple ways to help emotions move instead of staying trapped

None of this has to look dramatic.

Healing often happens through quiet acts of care. Sometimes it's placing one hand on your heart and breathing slowly. Sometimes it's letting tears come without apologizing for them. You might gently stretch your arms or neck, shake out your hands, write what you're feeling without editing yourself, or sit in silence for a few minutes.

Even two minutes of emotional presence can shift your nervous system.

It sends a simple message to your body: *I'm listening.*

Psychologically, this kind of gentle attention helps emotions move instead of staying trapped. You're not trying to fix what you feel — you're allowing it to exist. And that permission alone creates space for release.

Small moments like these add up.

They teach your body that it's safe to feel again.

And that's where healing begins.

Emotional boundaries matter

Not everyone needs access to your healing.

Some people minimize what you're going through. Some rush you toward feeling better. Some avoid the topic altogether because they don't know how to sit with pain. And while that can be hurtful, you're allowed to protect your emotional space.

Emotional safety might sound like quietly saying, *"I'm not ready to talk about that,"* or *"I need quiet today."* Sometimes it's letting someone know, *"That comment wasn't helpful."* You don't have to explain yourself beyond that. Psychologically, setting boundaries is part of rebuilding safety after loss — it teaches your nervous system that you are allowed to choose what feels supportive.

This isn't selfish.

It's self-respect.

You're learning how to care for yourself in a new way.

And that matters.

Take a moment and reflect with me

Ask yourself:
- What emotion shows up most often lately?
- Where do I feel it in my body?
- What helps me feel emotionally safer?
- What do I need more of right now — space, connection, or rest?

Write whatever comes.

Let honesty lead.

Here are some simple but effective daily practices to build emotional safety

Choose one.

That's enough.
- Check in with yourself each morning: "What am I feeling?"
- Take three slow breaths when emotions rise
- Name your feelings instead of judging them
- Create one quiet moment in your day
- End the day by acknowledging one emotion you honored

Consistency matters more than intensity.

Let's complete this quick but gentle practice

Close your eyes.

Place one hand on your chest.

Take a slow breath.

Say quietly:
> *My emotions are allowed here.*
> *I am safe to feel.*
> *I don't have to rush my healing.*

Come back to this practice anytime you feel you need or want to.

Emotional thriving doesn't mean you stop hurting. It means you stop abandoning yourself when you hurt. It means learning how to hold your feelings with compassion. And that changes everything.

Chapter 12

Physical Thriving: Learning How to Live in Your Body Again

"Your body remembers what your heart has been holding."

Let's talk about your body for a moment.

Grief doesn't only live in your heart or your mind. It settles into your muscles, your stomach, your chest, your energy levels, and your sleep. A lot of people don't realize this at first. They just know they feel tired in a way that rest doesn't seem to fix.

If that's you, I want you to hear this gently:

Your body has been carrying more than you realize.

Psychologically and physically, grief asks your system to stay alert, to hold tension, to keep going even when everything feels heavy. That kind of endurance takes a toll. What you're feeling isn't imagined. It's your body responding to loss in the only way it knows how.

And now, as you begin to notice it, you're already taking the first step toward healing.

Your body deserves the same compassion you've been offering your heart.

Slowly. Kindly. One moment at a time.

Here's what's really happening physically after loss

When you experience grief or prolonged emotional stress, your body goes into survival mode.

Your nervous system releases stress hormones like cortisol and adrenaline — the same chemicals designed to help you escape danger. In short bursts, they're helpful. They get you through emergencies. But grief isn't a quick event. It lingers. And when loss stretches on, those hormones can stay elevated longer than they're meant to.

Research in psychoneuroimmunology — the study of how the mind, body, and immune system are connected — shows that prolonged grief can affect sleep, digestion, immune function, muscle tension, inflammation, and overall energy levels. That's why grief so often shows up physically. You may feel deeply tired, notice aches and pains, experience stomach issues or headaches, feel tightness in your chest, breathe more shallowly, or see changes in appetite and restlessness.

None of this means something is wrong with you.

It means your body has been protecting you.

Your system has been working overtime to help you survive something meaningful. These sensations aren't signs of weakness — they're signs that your body has been carrying a lot.

And now, slowly, gently, it's allowed to rest.

Healing doesn't happen by pushing these sensations away. It happens when you begin meeting your body with understanding instead of frustration. When you recognize that every symptom tells a story — not of failure, but of endurance.

Your body remembers what you've been through.

And with time, safety, and compassion, it can learn how to soften again.

Physical thriving begins with compassion, not discipline

After grief, many people instinctively try to fix their body.

They push harder. They criticize themselves. They tell themselves they just need more willpower. But healing doesn't begin with force — it begins with listening. Your body doesn't need punishment. It needs safety. It needs gentleness. It needs consistency.

Psychologically, when the nervous system has been through trauma, it responds far better to compassion than pressure. Real physical thriving isn't about getting your old body back. That version of you lived in a different season. This is about learning how to care for the body you're in now — the one that's been carrying loss, adapting, and doing its best to keep you going.

Let yourself meet your body with kindness.

Healing happens when you replace self-criticism with care.

Slowly. Patiently. In your own time.

You may feel disconnected from your body — and that's normal

After loss, many people begin to feel physically disconnected from themselves.

You might stop noticing hunger or push past fatigue. You may find yourself ignoring pain or moving through the day on autopilot, treating your body more like a machine than a living, feeling system. This isn't because you don't care about yourself — it's because dissociation is a common trauma response. When things feel overwhelming, your nervous system sometimes pulls you away from physical sensation as a form of protection.

There's nothing wrong with you for experiencing this.

Reconnecting with your body doesn't happen all at once. It happens in small moments of awareness — noticing your breath, feeling your feet on the floor, pausing when you're tired, recognizing when you need water or rest. Each gentle check-in helps your system remember that it's safe to be present again.

You don't have to force this process.

Just allow it to unfold slowly.

Your body has been holding a lot.

And it's allowed to come back into connection at its own pace.

Let me share something important

You don't need intense workouts or perfect routines to heal your body.

Your nervous system responds best to:
- Gentle movement
- Predictable rhythms
- Nourishment
- Rest
- Breath

These signal safety.

And safety is what allows healing.

Here are gentle ways to support your body right now

As you begin caring for your body after loss, I want to gently remind you to choose what feels manageable — not impressive. Manageable.

Grief takes a toll on the body in quiet ways. Stress burns through energy and minerals, and many people don't realize how dehydrating grief can be. Sometimes the most supportive place to start is simply with water. Even one extra glass a day can help your nervous system feel a little steadier. It's a small act of care that tells your body you're paying attention.

Movement doesn't have to look like exercise right now. Your body just needs reminders that it's still here. That might be stretching your arms, walking for a few minutes, rolling your shoulders, or gently swaying to music. These soft movements send a simple message to your system: I'm alive. They help release stored tension and bring you back into your body without forcing anything.

You may also notice waves of fatigue — or the opposite, a wired restlessness that makes it hard to settle. Both are common after loss. Sleep often becomes disrupted when your nervous system is on high alert. If you're tired, allow yourself to rest. If you feel wired, slow breathing can help signal safety. Creating calming nighttime rituals — dimming the lights, sipping warm tea, listening to quiet music, taking a few deep breaths — gives your body cues that it's okay to soften. Over time, repetition teaches your system how to unwind again.

Eating may feel different too. Grief affects appetite in all kinds of ways. Some people eat more. Some eat less. There is no right way here. Try to focus on nourishment instead of perfection. Warm meals, simple foods, and protein when you can. Your body needs fuel to heal, even when hunger feels distant.

None of this has to be done perfectly.

Just gently.

Your body has been carrying a lot.

And every small moment of kindness you offer it matters.

Take a moment and reflect with me

Ask yourself:
- Where do I feel tension in my body lately?
- What does my body need more of right now — rest, movement, or nourishment?
- How have I been treating my body since my loss?

Write whatever comes.

No judgment.

Just awareness.

Here are some simple but effective daily practices to restore energy and reconnect with your body

Pick one or two.

That's enough.

- Drink a glass of water when you wake up
- Take five slow breaths before meals
- Stretch for two minutes in the morning or evening
- Step outside once a day

- **Place your hand on your chest when you feel overwhelmed**
- **Go to bed ten minutes earlier**

Small actions create safety.

Safety creates healing.

Let's complete this quick but gentle practice

Place one hand on your chest and one on your belly.

Take a slow breath in through your nose.

Let it out through your mouth.

Do this three times.

Then say quietly:
> *My body has carried me through so much.*
> *I choose to treat it with kindness.*
> *Healing is happening, even now.*

Come back to this practice anytime you feel you need or want to.

Physical thriving doesn't mean your body will never hurt again. It means you stop fighting your body. It means you begin listening. It means learning how to live inside yourself with compassion. And that matters more than anything.

Chapter 13

Spiritual Thriving:
Finding Meaning and Connection Again

"You don't have to have answers. Honesty is enough."

Let's talk about something that often feels complicated after loss — your spirit.

Grief can affect faith in many different ways. For some people, it deepens their connection. For others, it shakes everything. You might feel closer to God one moment and angry the next. You may feel abandoned, stop praying, start questioning, or find yourself unsure of what you believe anymore. All of this is more common than people talk about.

If any of that feels familiar, I want you to know you're not alone.

Spiritual grief is real. And it deserves the same tenderness and compassion as emotional or physical grief. Psychologically, loss disrupts our sense of meaning and connection, so it makes sense that your spiritual world would feel unsettled too. There's nothing wrong with you for experiencing this.

You don't have to have clarity right now.

You don't have to force belief.

Just allow yourself to be where you are.

Healing begins when you let your spirit breathe again.

Here's something important most people don't say out loud

Loss doesn't only take people.

It takes certainty. It takes trust. It takes your sense of safety in the world. And when that happens, it naturally reaches into your spiritual life too. You may notice questions surfacing where confidence once lived, or distance where connection used to feel easy.

Psychological and spiritual research both show that grief often disrupts a person's sense of meaning, purpose, and connection. Even people with deep faith experience seasons of doubt, anger, or confusion after loss. That doesn't mean your faith is weak. It means your heart is trying to understand something that doesn't make sense.

There's nothing wrong with you for feeling this way.

Spiritual thriving doesn't begin with answers.

It begins with honesty.

With letting yourself admit what hurts. With naming what feels broken. With allowing space for questions instead of rushing toward certainty. Healing starts when you tell the truth about where you are — not where you think you should be.

And from that honesty, something gentle begins to grow again.

You're allowed to feel whatever you feel toward God, life, or the universe

You may notice a whole range of feelings rising up when it comes to God, life, or the universe.

Anger. Confusion. Distance. Longing. Gratitude. Silence. Sometimes all of it at once.

Many people carry quiet shame around these emotions. Thoughts like, *I shouldn't be mad at God,* or *I should have more faith,* or *I shouldn't be questioning things* can start to creep in. But spiritual healing doesn't begin with pretending. It begins with honesty.

You don't have to perform belief.

You don't have to hide your pain.

Psychologically, healing happens when emotions are allowed instead of suppressed. Whatever you're feeling right now belongs. Your grief doesn't disqualify you from connection — it's part of it.

There is room for your anger.

There is room for your doubt.

There is room for your hope.

Let yourself bring your whole heart to this season. You don't need to clean it up first.

Spiritual thriving is about connection, not perfection

This matters.

Spiritual thriving isn't about having everything figured out. It's about reconnecting — with yourself, with something greater, and with meaning. After loss, that connection may feel different than it once did, and that's okay. Your spiritual path is allowed to evolve.

For some people, reconnection comes through prayer or meditation. For others, it shows up in nature, journaling, music, scripture, quiet moments, or deep conversations that open the heart. There is no single right way. What matters is finding what feels grounding and true for you.

Your spirituality after grief may not look the same as it did before.

That doesn't make it wrong.

It makes it real.

Healing doesn't require perfection. It asks only for honesty, presence, and a willingness to stay connected — even when the answers aren't clear. And in that connection, something steady begins to grow again.

Let me share something gentle

Many people wait until they feel "spiritual enough" to reconnect.

But connection doesn't come after healing.

It comes during it.

You don't need the right words.

You don't need strong faith.

You just need presence.

Even sitting quietly and saying, "I don't understand this," counts.

Finding meaning after loss takes time

Grief often leaves you sitting with questions that feel bigger than words.

Why did this happen?
What am I supposed to do now?

Who am I becoming?

These are not questions with quick answers. Meaning doesn't arrive all at once after loss — it's rebuilt slowly, in quiet moments of reflection, in acts of service, in personal growth, and in the simple choice to keep living even when it feels hard.

Psychologists call this process *meaning-making* — the way we gradually create purpose after trauma. Research shows that people who gently explore meaning after loss often experience deeper resilience and emotional healing over time. Not because the pain disappears, but because they begin to weave what happened into their life story in a way that feels more whole.

You don't have to force this.

You don't have to figure it all out right now.

Meaning unfolds naturally when you give yourself permission to feel, to grow, and to stay open to becoming. Your story is still being written — and even in grief, there is space for purpose to take shape.

Slowly. Tenderly. In your own time.

Here are gentle ways to support your spiritual healing

As you tend to your spiritual healing, I want to remind you that this is a deeply personal journey. You're allowed to choose what resonates for you and gently leave the rest behind. There's no one right way to reconnect with your spirit after loss.

Sometimes healing begins in quiet moments. Even five minutes of silence can help your nervous system reset. Sitting, breathing, and simply being present — without an agenda — gives your body space to soften. These small pauses remind your system that it's safe to slow down.

You may also find comfort in speaking honestly, in whatever way feels natural. If you pray, let your prayers be real. If you journal, write what's actually on your heart. If you talk out loud, allow your words to come without filtering. You don't have to be polite with grief. Spiritual healing isn't about saying the right things — it's about telling the truth.

Nature can be a gentle companion in this process too. Trees, sunlight, water, fresh air — all of these help regulate the nervous system and quietly remind the body that life continues. Stepping outside when you can, even briefly, can bring grounding in ways that are hard to explain but easy to feel.

And don't underestimate the power of uplifting, grounding content. Music, meaningful words, scripture, or reflective messages that feel supportive — not overwhelming — can nourish your spirit when it feels tired. Just like your body and heart, your spirit needs care too.

Let this part of healing unfold slowly.

There's no rush.

Just gentle reconnection, one moment at a time.

Take a moment and reflect with me

Ask yourself:
- How has loss affected my faith or sense of meaning?
- What helps me feel spiritually connected, even a little?
- What questions am I carrying right now?

Write whatever comes.

There's no right way to do this.

Here are some simple but effective daily practices to reconnect spiritually

Pick one.

That's enough.

- Sit quietly for three minutes
- Say one honest prayer or affirmation
- Step outside and take five slow breaths
- Write one sentence about what you're grateful for
- Read something that brings comfort
- Light a candle and sit in silence

These small moments build spiritual safety.

Let's complete this quick but gentle practice

Close your eyes.

Take a slow breath.

Place one hand on your heart.

Say quietly:
>*I don't have to understand everything right now.*
>*I am allowed to question and believe.*
>*I am still connected to life.*

Come back to this practice anytime you feel you need or want to.

Spiritual thriving doesn't mean you never doubt. It means you keep showing up. It means you allow space for meaning to grow again. And that's more than enough.

Chapter 14

Financial Thriving:
Learning How to Feel Safe With Money Again

"Safety comes before strategy. Your nervous system needs reassurance before your budget needs structure."

Let's talk about something many people quietly carry after loss.

Money.

Not in a judgmental way. Not in a "get rich" way. But in a deeply human way.

Because grief doesn't only break hearts — it disrupts your sense of financial safety too. For many people, money becomes another layer of anxiety added to everything they're already holding. Bills feel heavier. Decisions feel scarier. The future feels less certain.

If you've noticed yourself feeling stressed, fearful, overwhelmed, or emotionally disconnected when it comes to finances since your loss, I want you to know this: you're not imagining it.

This experience has a name.

It's called money grief.

And it's real.

Psychologically, loss can shake your sense of stability, making anything tied to survival — including finances — feel more intense. Your nervous system starts looking for security, and money naturally becomes part of that equation. There's nothing wrong with you for feeling this way. Your body is responding to something deeply destabilizing.

And just like every other part of grief, this deserves gentleness, understanding, and care.

You don't have to face it alone.

And healing your relationship with money is possible — slowly, compassionately, and in your own time.

Here's what often happens financially after loss

Loss has a way of touching every part of your life — including your finances.

It can change income. It can shift priorities. It can affect spending, energy, and confidence. And even if your financial situation hasn't dramatically changed on paper, your relationship with money often does. That's because grief doesn't stay in one place. It moves through your whole system.

Psychologically, grief and trauma activate the brain's threat response. When emotional safety feels compromised, your nervous system starts scanning for danger everywhere — including around money. That's why financial thoughts may feel louder now. That's why budgeting can feel harder. That's why planning for the future might suddenly feel overwhelming.

Your nervous system isn't chasing luxury.

It's searching for stability.

It's looking for safety.

Understanding this can soften self-judgment. You're not failing at finances. Your body is trying to protect you after something deeply destabilizing happened. And once you begin restoring that sense of safety — gently and consistently — your relationship with money can start to feel calmer again.

One small step at a time.

Money grief doesn't always look like debt

Sometimes money grief looks like:
- Fear of opening bank apps
- Avoiding bills
- Impulse spending for comfort
- Freezing instead of making financial decisions
- Feeling guilty about purchases
- Feeling scared to invest in yourself
- Feeling behind

These are not character flaws.

They are trauma responses.

Your system is trying to protect you from more loss.

Financial thriving starts with safety, not strategy

Most financial advice jumps straight to numbers.

But after grief, what you really need first is emotional safety.

Before budgets. Before goals. Before planning.

Loss shakes your sense of security, and when your nervous system doesn't feel safe, even simple financial tasks can feel overwhelming. That's not because you lack discipline — it's because your body is still trying to protect you. Stability doesn't come from forcing yourself into systems you're not ready for. It comes from gently helping your nervous system feel secure again.

That's the foundation.

When safety comes first, everything else becomes easier to build.
Clarity follows.
Confidence returns.
Small steps start to feel possible.

Financial thriving doesn't begin with strategy.

It begins with feeling held enough to take the next breath.

And from there, you can grow — slowly, kindly, and in your own time.

Let me say something important

You do not have to have everything figured out financially right now.

You do not have to be perfect with money.

You do not have to fix everything at once.

Stability is built slowly.

One small choice at a time.

Rebuilding financial stability begins with awareness

Rebuilding financial stability often begins with something very simple: awareness.

Not awareness rooted in judgment — but in curiosity. Gently looking at your money, just noticing what's there. That might look like checking your bank balance, writing down your monthly expenses, noticing where your income comes from, or observing your spending patterns. There's no fixing required in this moment. Just seeing. Psychologically, awareness restores a sense of control after loss. When you allow yourself to look without shame, you take the first step toward feeling grounded again.

From there, structure can begin to form naturally — and I want you to know this isn't about restriction. It's about safety. Structure helps your nervous system relax because it reduces uncertainty. Something as simple as listing your bills, sketching out a rough monthly outline, setting one small savings goal, or automating a single payment can make a meaningful difference. These tiny systems gently reduce mental load. They free up emotional energy. They tell your brain, *there's a plan here, even if it's still taking shape.*

You don't need a perfect budget.

You don't need everything organized overnight.

You just need small moments of clarity.

And those moments, over time, become stability.

Let's talk about rebuilding confidence with money

Grief has a way of making everything feel fragile — especially when it comes to money.

You may notice yourself questioning your decisions or feeling afraid of making mistakes. That's not because you suddenly became bad with finances. It's because loss disrupts your sense of control and safety, and your nervous system is trying to protect you from more harm. Financial confidence often takes a hit after grief.

But here's something gentle and true: confidence doesn't return through big leaps.

It comes back through small wins.

Paying one bill.
Saving ten dollars.
Making one intentional purchase.

Each small action sends a quiet message to your nervous system: *I can handle this.* And that matters more than you might realize. Psychologically, these tiny moments of agency help rebuild trust in yourself. They remind your body that you are capable, present, and moving forward — even when things still feel tender.

You don't have to become fearless with money.

You just have to keep showing yourself, one small step at a time, that you are still here and still capable.

And that is how confidence grows again.

Learning how to feel safe with finances again

As you learn how to feel safe with finances again, I want to remind you to start with what feels doable — not overwhelming.

Real financial safety doesn't come from having millions. It comes from predictability. From knowing what's coming in and what's going out. From having even a tiny cushion. From having some kind of plan, even if it's loose and evolving. Psychologically, our nervous system feels calmer when there's clarity. Studies in financial psychology show that people experience less anxiety when they feel informed and organized, regardless of income level. It isn't the amount of money that creates peace — it's understanding and awareness.

That's why small moments of checking in with your finances matter so much. Not from fear. From care. Each time you look, each time you name what's there, each time you make a gentle adjustment, you're telling your body, *I'm paying attention. I'm taking care of myself.*

And that builds safety.

Slowly. Quietly. One small step at a time.

You don't need perfection.
 You don't need everything figured out.

You just need presence.

And that is already within your reach.

Here are gentle ways to support your financial healing

As you begin tending to your finances after loss, I want to remind you of something gentle: you don't have to do everything at once.

Start with what feels doable. Not overwhelming. Healing your relationship with money isn't about big, dramatic changes — it's about small moments of presence. You might choose one simple ritual each week, maybe just ten quiet minutes where you sit with your finances. You could light a candle, play soft music, and gently look at your accounts. Not to judge yourself. Just to meet your money where it is. Over time, this shifts money from something you avoid into something you can approach with calm.

You may notice emotions rising when you do this — anxiety, fear, even shame. That's normal. Money often holds a lot of emotional weight, especially after loss. The key isn't to wait until those feelings disappear. It's to let them exist while you still take small, steady steps forward. Emotion can be present, but it doesn't get to run the system. You do. Each tiny action helps rebuild a sense of control and safety.

Even creating the smallest emergency cushion can make a difference. Setting aside $5 or $10 may not seem significant on the surface, but psychologically it sends a powerful message to your nervous system: I am taking care of myself. Small reserves matter. They create a sense of grounding and preparedness, one gentle layer at a time.

And I want to say this clearly: you are allowed to receive.

Whether that looks like accepting help, using discounts, accessing assistance, or opening yourself to new opportunities — receiving is part of healing too. You don't have to carry everything alone. Letting support in doesn't mean you're weak. It means you're honoring your humanity.

Financial healing isn't about perfection.

It's about rebuilding trust with yourself.

Slowly. Kindly. One small choice at a time.

Take a moment and reflect with me

Ask yourself:
- How has grief changed my relationship with money?
- What feels hardest financially right now?

- What would make me feel even slightly safer?

Write whatever comes. No shame. Just honesty.

Here are some simple but effective daily practices to rebuild financial confidence

Pick one.
That's enough.

- Check your bank balance once a day without judgment
- Save one small amount this week
- Write down one financial goal
- Open one bill instead of avoiding it
- Say out loud: "I am rebuilding stability."

These small actions compound.

Let's complete this quick but gentle practice

Place one hand on your chest.

Take a slow breath.

Say quietly:
> *I am learning how to feel safe again.*
> *My financial healing matters.*
> *Small steps are enough.*

Come back to this practice anytime you feel you need or want to.

Financial thriving doesn't mean you'll never feel stress again. It means you stop avoiding your finances. It means you rebuild trust in yourself. It means you learn how to create stability after loss.

And that is powerful.

Chapter 15

Relationships After Loss:
Learning How to Love in a New Way

"Grief changes how you love — not because you're cold, but because you've learned what matters."

Let's talk about relationships.

Because grief doesn't just change how you feel. It changes how you connect.

You may not recognize yourself around other people anymore. You may feel distant, guarded, or emotionally tired. You may crave connection and also want to be left alone. And if that sounds familiar, I want you to know:

You're not broken. Your heart has been protecting itself.

Here's what often happens to relationships after loss

Loss reshapes your nervous system.

It changes your tolerance for noise, drama, and surface-level interactions. It often makes you more sensitive. More selective. More aware of what matters.

Psychologists call this relational recalibration — the natural shift that happens when trauma or grief changes your priorities and emotional capacity.

That's why:
Some friendships fade. Some deepen. Some feel awkward. Some no longer fit.

This is not a failure. It's growth.

When friendships change

As you move through grief, you may begin to notice changes in the people around you.

Some may disappear. Others may show up in ways you didn't expect. Some avoid the topic altogether, while others say the wrong thing or try to fix your pain. Some simply don't know how to sit with it. All of this can be deeply hurtful, especially when you're already carrying so much.

But I want you to hear this clearly: it doesn't mean you are too much.

Grief has a way of revealing emotional limits — not just yours, but other people's too. Many people care deeply, but they don't always know how to support something they haven't experienced themselves. Psychologically, when faced with pain they don't understand, people often retreat, minimize, or move into problem-solving mode because discomfort feels unsafe to them.

That doesn't make your grief smaller.

It just explains their behavior.

And you're allowed to grieve these changes too. You're allowed to mourn relationships that shifted, conversations that never happened, and support that didn't show up the way you hoped. That's part of this journey — not a side story, but a real layer of loss that deserves acknowledgment.

Be gentle with yourself as you navigate these changes.

You're learning who can walk with you now.

And that matters.

Parenting while grieving

If you're a parent, grief adds another layer to everything.

You're carrying your own emotions while still showing up for your children, and that can feel overwhelming. You may notice guilt creeping in because you don't have the same energy you once did, or worry about how your grief might be affecting them. Those thoughts are heavy — and they're also very human.

Let me say this gently: you don't need to be perfect.

You just need to be honest and present.

Children don't need you to hide your emotions. In fact, seeing you feel — and then regulate those feelings — teaches them something important about being human. Psychologically, kids learn emotional safety by watching how the adults around them move through hard moments. When they see that sadness can be named, held, and eventually softened, it helps them feel safer with their own emotions too.

Sometimes it's the simplest things that matter most. Letting them know it's okay to feel sad. Answering their questions in ways they can understand. Keeping familiar routines when you're able. Offering hugs, reassurance, and quiet presence. These small acts build security far more than pretending everything is fine.

Your presence matters more than your performance.

You don't have to have all the answers. You don't have to carry this flawlessly.

Just showing up — as you are — is already enough.

Dating after loss (if this applies to you)

Dating after loss can feel deeply confusing.

One day you may feel open to connection, and the next you might feel completely closed off. You may notice waves of guilt when you think about moving forward, or find that attraction feels distant or unfamiliar. All of this is normal. Your heart has been through something profound, and it makes sense that intimacy would feel different now.

There's no timeline for reopening yourself to love.

You don't have to rush back into closeness. You don't owe anyone an explanation for where you are emotionally. Psychologically, grief can temporarily quiet desire as your nervous system focuses on safety and recovery — this isn't something to fix, it's something to honor.

And when you do begin to consider dating again, I want you to remember this: allowing someone new into your life doesn't mean replacing what you lost. It doesn't erase your past or diminish the love you already carry. It simply means making room for connection in a new chapter.

And that chapter gets to unfold slowly.

With honesty.
With boundaries.
With tenderness.

Let yourself move at the pace your heart understands.

Learning how to love again — in a different way

Loss has a way of changing how you love.

You may notice that your heart feels different now — more cautious in some ways, but also deeper and more honest. You might find that you have less patience for surface-level connections and more desire for emotional safety than excitement. What once felt important may not carry the same weight anymore, and what truly matters feels clearer.

This isn't coldness.

It's wisdom.

Grief often reshapes our priorities because it reminds us how fragile life is and how meaningful connection really is. Psychologically, this is part of how we adapt after loss — your nervous system begins seeking safety, authenticity, and depth instead of novelty or distraction. You're not becoming closed off. You're becoming more discerning.

Grief teaches you what matters.

It teaches you to value presence over performance.
Depth over convenience.
Honesty over comfort.

And as you learn to love in this new way, give yourself permission to honor it. Your heart is not smaller.

It's wiser.

Emotional boundaries become essential

After loss, your emotional energy becomes something sacred.

You may notice that you don't have the same capacity you once did

— for conversations, for explanations, for other people's expectations. That's not weakness. That's your nervous system protecting itself while you heal. Not everyone needs access to your inner world right now, and you're allowed to honor that.

Boundaries can feel uncomfortable at first, especially if you're used to being the strong one or the accommodating one. But gentle boundaries aren't about shutting people out — they're about taking care of yourself. Sometimes that looks like quietly saying, *"I'm not ready to talk about that,"* or *"I need space today."* Sometimes it sounds like, *"That doesn't feel supportive,"* or simply, *"I'm protecting my peace right now."* You don't have to over-explain. Your needs are reason enough.

It helps to think of boundaries not as walls, but as filters. Walls block everything. Filters allow what's nourishing to pass through while keeping what feels overwhelming at a distance. Boundaries let you stay open to connection without losing yourself in the process. Psychologically, this is part of rebuilding emotional safety — teaching your body and heart that you're allowed to choose what feels supportive.

And here's something I want you to hold close:

You don't need a large circle.

You need a safe one.

Even one person who listens without trying to fix you.
One person who shows up.
One person who lets you be real.

That is enough.

Grief has a way of clarifying what matters — and who matters. Let yourself gravitate toward the people who meet you with softness, patience, and presence. Let your world become smaller if it needs to for a while. Healing doesn't require a crowd.

It just requires honesty, safety, and space to be exactly where you are.

And you are allowed all of that.

Here are gentle ways to support your relationships after loss

As you move through relationships after loss, I want to remind you of something important: you don't have to do this perfectly.

You're allowed to choose what resonates for you. You're allowed to show up honestly, even if you don't have the energy to explain everything. Sometimes simple truth is enough. Saying something like, *"I'm having a hard week,"* or *"I'm not myself right now,"* can communicate what you need without requiring you to relive your story. You don't owe anyone details. Your feelings are valid even when they're shared quietly.

You may also notice that not everyone will meet you where you are. Some people may pull away. Some may say the wrong thing. Some may disappear entirely. That hurts — and it's okay to acknowledge that pain. But over time, learning to release expectations can help protect your heart. Not everyone has the capacity to walk beside you through grief, and that isn't always a reflection of your worth. Sometimes it's simply a reflection of where they are in their own lives.

Connection still matters, though. Healing happens in relationship.

When you feel ready, you might begin reaching out intentionally —
toward people who feel safe, who listen without fixing, who allow
you to be exactly as you are. That might look like leaning into one
trusted friend, joining a support space where loss is understood, or
slowly opening yourself to new connections when your heart feels
ready. There's no timeline for this. Just gentle noticing of who feels
supportive now.

You don't have to rebuild your social world all at once.

You don't have to force closeness.

Let connection unfold naturally.

Trust that the right people — the ones who can hold your truth —
will find their way into your life, sometimes in familiar faces, and
sometimes in unexpected ones.

And remember: you are allowed to protect your energy while still
remaining open to love.

Both can exist at the same time.

Take a moment and reflect with me

Ask yourself:
- Which relationships feel nourishing right now?
- Which feel draining?
- What do I need more of — space or connection?
- How has grief changed what I value in relationships?

Write whatever comes.

Let honesty guide you.

Here are some simple but effective daily practices to rebuild connection

Pick one.

That's enough.

- Send one honest text
- Share how you're really doing with someone safe
- Spend five minutes fully present with your child or pet
- Set one boundary
- Say no when you need to

Small actions shape emotional safety.

Let's complete this quick but gentle practice

Place one hand on your heart.

Take a slow breath.

Say quietly:

> *I am allowed to love in my own time.*
> *My relationships are evolving.*
> *I deserve connection that feels safe.*

Come back to this practice anytime you feel you need or want to.

Relationships after loss don't return to what they were. They become something new. And that new doesn't have to be lonely. It just has to be honest.

PART SIX: BECOMING WHO GRIEF SHAPED YOU TO BE

Chapter 16

You Are Not Who You Were
(And That's Okay)

"There is no going back. There is only becoming."

Let's talk about something many people don't expect after grief.

You may not recognize yourself anymore.

Your reactions feel different. Your priorities have shifted. Things that once mattered don't carry the same weight, and things you used to tolerate suddenly feel heavy. You might notice you need more rest, more quiet, or more emotional space. You may feel more sensitive, more selective, or more aware of what truly matters.

And somewhere in all of this, a quiet question may surface:

Who am I now?

If that question has crossed your mind, I want you to know this is a normal part of healing.

Loss changes identity. Not because you're weak — but because something meaningful reshaped your inner world.

Psychologists call this identity disruption. When you experience a major loss, your sense of self is affected because your roles, routines, relationships, and expectations for the future all shift at once. Your brain and nervous system are forced to reorganize around a new reality. You are adapting to a world that no longer looks the same, and adaptation always brings change. So if you feel different, it's because you are. And that doesn't mean something went wrong. It means growth is happening, even if it feels uncomfortable.

Many people try to "get back to normal" after grief. They want to feel like themselves again. But here's the truth most people don't tell you: there is no going back. There is only becoming.

You don't return to your old self after loss. You integrate what happened and evolve. Trying to be who you were before grief often creates frustration, because that version of you existed in a different reality.

You are allowed to become someone new. You are allowed to change.

This is where guilt sometimes enters.

You may feel guilty for growing. For outgrowing people. For wanting more. For laughing again. For dreaming again. But growth is not betrayal. Healing is not disrespect. Moving forward does not mean forgetting. You carry what you lost with you. And you are still allowed to expand.

Grief can also strip away confidence. You may find yourself questioning your decisions, doubting your strength, or feeling unsure of your direction. This happens because trauma disrupts your sense of control and safety. But confidence doesn't return through big achievements. It comes back through small choices — showing up, setting boundaries, honoring your needs, doing one hard thing at a time. Every small act rebuilds trust in yourself.

Let me share something gentle: you don't have to define who you are right now. You don't need a new identity immediately. You are allowed to be in between. Becoming takes time. And in-between seasons are sacred.

If you're open to it, start noticing what matters to you now. What feels nourishing? What feels draining? Your values may have shifted, and that's okay. Honor your limits. You don't have to do what you used to do.

Rest is wisdom. Try new things slowly — a new routine, a new interest, a new way of caring for yourself. Small exploration helps your sense of self grow again.

Take a moment and reflect with me.

- What feels different about you now?
- What have you learned about yourself through grief?
- What parts of you feel stronger?
- What parts need gentleness?

Write whatever comes. There is no right answer.

Here are a few simple ways to support identity healing in your everyday life. You don't need to do all of them — just choose one when you can.

- Speak kindly to yourself in the mirror.
- Say no when something feels wrong.
- Say yes when something feels supportive.
- Spend five minutes doing something just for you.
- Write one sentence about who you're becoming

These small actions rebuild self-trust over time.

Let's complete a quick but gentle practice together.

Place one hand on your heart.

Take a slow breath.

Say quietly:
> *I am allowed to change.*

I am becoming someone new.
And that is okay.

Come back to this practice anytime you feel you need or want to.

You are not who you were. And that doesn't mean you lost yourself. It means you are evolving.

Grief reshapes us. But it can also deepen us. And who you are becoming matters.

Chapter 17

Creating Your New Normal

"You are allowed to redesign your life around who you are now."

After loss, life doesn't return to what it was.

And that can feel unsettling.

You may wake up one day and realize that your routines feel different. Your energy has changed. The way you move through your days isn't the same anymore. Things that once felt automatic now require effort. Things that once brought comfort may not anymore.

This is part of grief.

Loss doesn't just take people or moments.

It reshapes daily life.

So if everything feels unfamiliar, you're not doing anything wrong. You're learning how to live in a new reality.

Psychologists sometimes call this life reconstruction — the process of rebuilding routines, roles, and meaning after major loss. Your brain and nervous system are adjusting to a world that no longer matches the one you were living in before. That adjustment takes time. There is no rush. There is only rebuilding.

And rebuilding doesn't happen all at once.

It happens slowly, in ordinary moments.

Many people try to force themselves back into their old routines. They think if they just go back to doing what they used to do, everything will feel normal again. But here's the truth most people don't tell you: your old normal doesn't exist anymore. And that doesn't mean your future is broken. It means you get to create something new.

A new normal doesn't arrive fully formed. It's built through small choices, trial and error, and learning what supports you now.

Let me share something gentle. Your new normal doesn't have to look impressive. It doesn't have to be productive. It doesn't have to match anyone else's healing timeline. Your new normal just has to feel safe enough for you to exist inside.

That might mean simpler days. Earlier bedtimes. Fewer commitments. More quiet. More boundaries. Different priorities.

That's not weakness.

That's wisdom.

Grief also changes your capacity. You may notice that you can't do as much as you used to. You get tired faster. You need more emotional space. You're less tolerant of chaos or negativity. Trauma research shows that prolonged stress lowers your tolerance for stimulation while increasing your need for predictability and rest. So if you feel overwhelmed more easily now, that isn't a character flaw.

It's your body asking for gentleness.

Creating your new normal often begins with small rhythms. Not rigid schedules. Gentle anchors. Things you can count on, even when everything else feels uncertain. Waking up around the same time. Drinking water in the morning. Stepping outside. Eating regular meals. Going to bed with intention.

These small consistencies quietly tell your nervous system: life is still happening. I am safe enough to participate.

Routines don't control you.

They support you.

Boundaries become just as important.

After loss, your energy is precious. You may need to say no more often. You may need to limit certain conversations. You may need to protect your time. You are allowed to redesign your life in ways that honor your healing.

Boundaries might sound like: I don't have the capacity for that right now. I need more rest. I'm choosing peace today.

These aren't selfish statements.

They are acts of self-respect.

Dreams also change after grief. Some dreams disappear. Some feel distant. Some become quieter. You may not feel ready to dream big again, and that's okay. Dreaming can start small. Better sleep. More peace. A calm home. A healthy body. A meaningful connection.

These are dreams too.

And they matter.

If you're open to it, take a moment and reflect with me.

- What does your life need more of right now? Less of?
- What feels supportive?

- **What feels draining?**
- **What would a gentle day look like for you?**

Write whatever comes. There are no right answers. Only your truth.

As you begin shaping your new normal, remember that you don't need a perfect plan. Just small, intentional choices.

- **Creating one daily anchor.**
- **Setting one boundary.**
- **Simplifying one part of your day.**
- **Adding one small moment of rest.**
- **Writing down one dream, even if it feels tiny.**

These small choices add up.

They become your personal thriving blueprint. Not a rigid plan — a living one. One that grows with you.

Let's pause for a quick but gentle practice.

Place one hand on your heart. Take a slow breath. Then say quietly:

I am allowed to rebuild my life slowly.
My new normal is taking shape.
I don't have to rush becoming.

Come back to this practice anytime you feel you need or want to.

Creating your new normal doesn't mean forgetting what you lost. It means learning how to live alongside it. It means giving yourself permission to design a life that supports who you are now.

And that is a powerful act of healing.

Chapter 18

Turning Pain Into Purpose

"Your story doesn't end with loss. It transforms through it."

There often comes a quiet moment in grief when you begin to wonder:

What do I do with everything I've been through?

Not in a dramatic way.

Just a soft, honest question.

You've survived something that changed you. You've felt the weight of loss. You've learned things about yourself you never wanted to learn this way. And somewhere inside, there may be a small desire to make sense of it all.

This is where purpose begins.

Not as a grand mission.

Not as pressure.

But as meaning slowly taking shape.

Psychologists call this meaning-making — the natural human process of trying to understand loss and integrate it into your life story. Research shows that people often begin to heal more deeply when they're able to find some sense of meaning after trauma, even if that meaning is quiet, personal, or still forming.

Purpose doesn't erase pain.

It helps you carry it.

Turning pain into purpose doesn't mean pretending everything happened for a reason. It doesn't mean forcing gratitude. It doesn't mean becoming inspirational before you're ready.

It simply means allowing your experiences to shape who you become.

You may notice that your heart feels more tender now. You might feel more compassionate toward others. You may have less tolerance for things that don't matter and more sensitivity to suffering. These shifts aren't accidental.

Grief often deepens empathy.

It widens perspective.

It changes what you care about.

And that is where purpose quietly lives.

Many people feel pressure to "do something big" with their pain. But purpose doesn't have to look impressive. It doesn't have to be public. It doesn't have to involve helping everyone.

Sometimes purpose looks like becoming more patient.

Sometimes it looks like being gentler with your children.

Sometimes it looks like checking on a friend.

Sometimes it looks like setting boundaries and choosing peace.

Sometimes it looks like simply continuing to live.

Service doesn't always mean volunteering or starting organizations. Service can be how you show up in everyday moments. It can be listening without fixing. It can be offering kindness when you know how heavy life can feel. It can be choosing compassion over judgment because you understand what invisible battles look like.

Your presence matters more than you realize.

Legacy also begins to shift after loss.

You may start thinking differently about how you want to live. About what you want to model. About what truly matters. Legacy isn't just what you leave behind someday — it's how you show up right now. It's the way you love. The way you speak. The way you care for yourself and others.

You don't have to be perfect to leave something meaningful.

You just have to be real.

Let me share something gentle.

You don't have to rush into purpose. You don't have to know what your story means yet.

Some seasons are for surviving. Some are for healing. Some are for becoming.

Purpose unfolds in its own time.

If you're open to it, take a moment and reflect with me.

- What has grief taught you about yourself?
- What feels more important now than it used to?
- Where do you feel drawn to be more gentle, more present, or

more intentional?
- What kind of person do you feel yourself becoming?

Write whatever comes.

There are no wrong answers.
Just truth.

As you move forward, remember that your purpose doesn't need to be loud. It can live in small choices. In everyday courage. In showing up even when it's hard. In honoring your story instead of hiding it.

Here are a few gentle ways to stay connected to purpose as it slowly forms.

- You might notice moments when your heart opens toward others. Let yourself follow that.
- You might feel called to share your story someday. Let that unfold naturally.
- You might feel inspired to support someone who's hurting. Trust that instinct.
- You might simply feel called to live more honestly. That matters too.

These are all expressions of purpose.

Let's pause for a quick but gentle practice.

Place one hand on your heart.

Take a slow breath.

Then say quietly:
My story matters.
I am allowed to grow from what I've been through.
Something meaningful is taking shape within me.

Come back to this practice anytime you feel you need or want to.

Turning pain into purpose doesn't mean your grief disappears. It means your experience becomes part of your wisdom. It means your heart learns how to hold both sorrow and meaning at the same time.

And that is a powerful way to live.

PART SEVEN: THRIVING IS YOUR BIRTHRIGHT

Chapter 19

Thriving Is Your Birthright

"You are still here. And that matters more than you know."

If you've made it this far in this book, I want to pause with you for
a moment.

Not to rush forward.

Not to summarize everything.

Just to acknowledge something important.

You have been through something that changed you.

You've carried grief.
You've learned how to survive.
You've begun rebuilding your inner world.
You've started becoming someone new.

That matters.

And now, here's something I want you to hear clearly:

You were not meant to only survive your life.

You were meant to live it.

Thriving isn't something reserved for people who haven't
experienced loss. It isn't a reward for being strong enough. It isn't
something you earn by healing perfectly.

Thriving is your birthright.

Grief may have interrupted your sense of safety. It may have
shaken your identity. It may have taken things you loved. But it did
not take your ability to experience peace again. It did not remove

your capacity for joy. It did not erase your worthiness of a full life.

Psychologically, humans are wired for resilience. Even after trauma, the nervous system is capable of regulation. The brain is capable of rewiring. The heart is capable of holding meaning alongside pain. This is called post-traumatic growth — the process through which people develop deeper awareness, compassion, purpose, and appreciation for life after hardship.

Not because the hardship was good.

But because humans are adaptive.

You are adaptive.

Thriving after loss doesn't mean your grief disappears. It means grief no longer drives the car. It means you learn how to carry what happened without letting it define everything that comes next. It means you begin to make choices from healing instead of survival.

You may notice that thriving looks quieter than you expected.

It might show up as waking up with less heaviness. It might feel like laughing without guilt. It might look like protecting your peace. It might be choosing healthier relationships. It might be honoring your body. It might be setting boundaries. It might be dreaming again.

Thriving doesn't arrive as a dramatic transformation.

It arrives in small, steady moments. One honest conversation. One boundary. One deep breath. One decision to care for yourself. Over time, those moments build a life.

Let me share something gentle.

You don't have to become a completely different person to thrive. You don't have to reinvent everything. You don't have to have a five-year plan.

Thriving begins when you start asking:

What supports me now?

Not what I *should* be doing. Not what others expect. What actually supports me. That question alone changes everything.

Practical thriving often looks like this:
- You notice when your nervous system is overwhelmed and you slow down.
- You choose routines that bring calm instead of chaos.
- You protect your energy.
- You let go of relationships that drain you.
- You allow rest.
- You nourish your body.
- You speak kindly to yourself.
- You create financial safety in small ways.
- You let emotions move instead of storing them.
- You reach out when you need support.
- You honor who you're becoming.

These aren't big spiritual ideas. These are daily acts of self-respect.

Thriving is not perfection.

It's presence. It's choosing to participate in your life again, even when it feels tender.

You may still have hard days.

You may still miss deeply.

You may still feel waves of sadness.

Thriving doesn't eliminate those. It gives you tools to meet them. And over time, the hard days no longer consume everything. They become part of a larger, richer picture.

If you're open to it, take a moment and reflect with me.

- What does thriving mean to you now?
  - Not before grief.
  - Now.
- What would feeling safe in your life look like?
- What would peace feel like in your body?
- What would a meaningful future include?

Write whatever comes.

Let this be your definition — not anyone else's.

Here are a few gentle ways to begin living from thriving instead of surviving:

- Start your day with one grounding breath.
- Make one choice that supports your well-being.
- Say no when something doesn't feel right.
- Say yes when something feels nourishing.
- Create moments of quiet.
- Celebrate small progress.
- Let yourself imagine again.

These are not small things. They are how you build a life.

Let's close with a gentle practice.

Place one hand on your heart.

Take a slow breath.

Then say quietly:
> *I am allowed to thrive.*
> *My life still holds meaning.*
> *I am moving forward with compassion.*

Come back to this practice anytime you feel you need or want to.

Grief may always be part of your story. But it does not get to write the ending.

You do.

And the future ahead of you still holds connection, growth, peace, and possibility.

You are not here just to survive what happened.

You are here to live.

And

Thriving is your Birthright.

BONUS SECTION

WHERE TO GO FROM HERE: A GENTLE RESOURCE GUIDE

Healing doesn't end when a book does.

This is just one part of your journey.

If you feel ready, here are gentle next steps you might consider.
Take what resonates and leave the rest.

You might choose to:

Seek professional support
A therapist, counselor, or grief specialist can provide a safe space to
process what you've been carrying.

Explore grief or support groups
Being in community with others who understand loss can reduce
isolation and normalize your experience.

Continue journaling
Writing helps integrate emotion, clarify thoughts, and release
stored grief.

Create grounding routines
Simple daily rhythms — walking, stretching, breathing, quiet time
— help regulate your nervous system.

Lean into safe connections
Even one supportive person makes a difference.

Learn more about grief and trauma
Understanding what's happening in your body and mind can bring
relief and validation.

Honor your healing in practical ways
Rest when you're tired. Nourish your body. Protect your energy.

Celebrate small progress.

And if right now all you can do is breathe and get through the day, that counts too.

There is no "right pace."

There is only your pace.

One Last Gentle Practice

Before you close this book, place one hand on your heart.

Take a slow breath.

Then say quietly:
> *I am still here.*
> *I am still becoming.*
> *And my future holds possibility.*

You don't have to know what comes next.

You just have to keep showing up.

With compassion.
With honesty.
With hope.

Your life is still unfolding.

And it is worthy of care.

SUPPORT BEYOND THESE PAGES

Before you close this book, I want to leave you with something practical.

Not because you're doing healing wrong.
Not because this journey requires fixing.

But because grief can feel overwhelming at times, and there may be moments when you need support beyond these pages.

That's human.

Some days reflection and self-care are enough.
Other days you may need another voice.
A trained professional.
A community that understands loss.
Immediate emotional support.

All of that is okay.

If you ever find yourself feeling unsafe, emotionally flooded, or in crisis, reaching out for immediate support can make a powerful difference. In the United States, you can call or text 988 to reach the 988 Suicide & Crisis Lifeline — available 24/7 with trained counselors who are there to listen, even if you're not sure what to say.

If you're outside the U.S., Befrienders Worldwide and the International Association for Suicide Prevention both provide international directories of crisis helplines by country.

If you feel ready for deeper healing, working with a therapist, counselor, or grief specialist can offer a safe, confidential space to process what you've been carrying. These directories can help you find licensed providers, many of whom offer virtual sessions:

- **Psychology Today** — searchable by location, specialty, and insurance
- **FindTreatment.gov** — a free U.S. treatment finder
- **Open Path Psychotherapy Collective** — reduced-fee options for those without adequate insurance

If your grief includes the loss of a beloved pet, please know this clearly: that loss matters. There are dedicated services for animal-related grief, created specifically for this kind of heartbreak:
- **Tufts Pet Loss Support Hotline**
- **Cornell Pet Loss Support Hotline**

These spaces exist so you don't have to explain why it hurts.

You may also find comfort in grief communities where people share openly and support one another through similar experiences. Sometimes it helps simply to be surrounded by others who understand, such as GriefShare or the educational community at What's Your Grief.

Some people find healing through reading and learning more about grief. If that feels supportive to you, a few widely respected books include *It's OK That You're Not OK* by Megan Devine, *Healing After Loss* by Martha Whitmore Hickman, and *Option B* by Sheryl Sandberg.

And for moments when emotions rise suddenly, having a simple grounding guide nearby — something that helps you slow your breathing, feel your body, and reconnect to the present — can be incredibly stabilizing. These tools don't remove grief, but they can help you ride the waves when they come. Even placing your feet on the floor, taking a few slow breaths, or resting a hand over your heart can remind your nervous system that you are safe right now.

Below this section, you'll also find journaling templates and a simple emergency grounding guide. These aren't assignments — just gentle supports you can return to whenever you need them.

You don't have to use everything.
 You don't have to need them all.

Just know they exist.

And most importantly:

You do not have to carry this alone.

Reaching for support is not weakness.

It's care.

JOURNALING TEMPLATES

Grab your favorite journal — or choose a new one to dedicate to this season of your healing.

There is no right way to use these pages.

You don't have to write every day.
You don't have to answer every prompt.
You don't have to make your words sound beautiful or organized.

Let this be a place where you tell the truth.

Some days you may write paragraphs.
Some days you may write one sentence.
Some days you may just sit with the questions.

That all counts.

Use these templates whenever you feel called — when emotions feel heavy, when your mind feels loud, when you need grounding, or when you simply want to check in with yourself.

This is not about doing it perfectly.

It's about creating space to feel, reflect, and gently reconnect with yourself.

Go at your own pace.

Your healing does not need to be rushed.

Daily Emotional Check-In
(Use anytime: morning, night, or when things feel heavy.)

Today feels like:

Right now, my body feels:

The emotions that are showing up:

Something that feels heavy:

Something that feels supportive (even a little):

One thing I need today:

A gentle truth I want to remember:

Naming Your Losses
(Because every loss matters.)

Today I'm acknowledging these losses:

What these losses changed for me:

The emotions that are showing up:

How my body reacts when I think about this:

What I wish people understood:

One way I can offer myself compassion today:

Survival to Thriving Reflection
(No judgment — just awareness.)

Right now, I feel more like:
☐ Surviving
☐ Somewhere in between
☐ Beginning to thrive

What survival looks like for me lately:

What thriving might look like (even in small ways):

One tiny step that feels doable:

Something I'm proud of myself for:

When My Mind Feels Loud
(For overthinking or emotional spirals.)

What's looping in my mind:

What I'm afraid of right now:

What I actually need in this moment:

A grounding thought I can return to:

"This is hard, and I'm allowed to take my time."

Becoming After Loss
(Identity healing.)

Who I was before:

Who I'm becoming:

Something grief has taught me:

Parts of me that feel stronger:

Parts of me that need gentleness:

One sentence about who I am now:

Gentle Gratitude (No Pressure)
(Not forced positivity — just noticing.)

One small thing I noticed today:

Something that brought even a moment of peace:

Something that helped me feel less alone:

FOR THE HARD WAVES

When Everything Feels Too Much

A Gentle Grounding Guide

Sometimes grief arrives without warning.

Your chest tightens.
Your thoughts race.
Your body feels overwhelmed.

If that's happening right now, pause with me.

You don't have to fix anything in this moment.

You don't have to understand what you're feeling.

You just need something steady to hold onto while the wave passes.

This guide is here to help you come back into your body and into the present moment — gently, slowly, and safely.

Step One: Breathe

Place one hand on your chest.

Take a slow breath in through your nose.

Let it out through your mouth.

Do that again.

You're here.

Step Two: Orient

Quietly name:
- 5 things you can see
- 4 things you can feel
- 3 things you can hear
- 2 things you can smell
- 1 thing you can taste or feel in your mouth

This tells your nervous system: I am safe right now.

Step Three: Feel Your Body

Press your feet into the floor.

Feel the chair or bed supporting you.

Gently squeeze your hands together.

Let your shoulders drop.

You don't have to disappear into the memory.

This moment is real.

Step Four: Speak Softly to Yourself

Say (out loud or in your mind):

"I am here."
"This will pass."
"I am safe enough right now."

These are not affirmations.

They are regulation.

Step Five: Anchor

Touch something grounding:
• jewelry
• a photo
• your skin
• a pillow
• the wall

Let your body remember the present.

Place one hand on your heart.

Take one slow breath.

Say:
"I survived something meaningful.
And I am still here."

If emotions feel overwhelming or unsafe:

• Reach out to someone you trust
• Contact a crisis line
• Seek professional help

Needing support is human.

You don't have to carry this alone.

Closing Author's Note

If you're reading this, it means you made it through something that changed you.

Maybe you read this book slowly.
Maybe you skipped around.
Maybe some chapters felt close to home while others didn't.

However you arrived here, I want you to know this:
You didn't come this far by accident.

Grief asks a lot of us. It asks us to feel things we never wanted to feel. It asks us to sit with uncertainty. It asks us to become someone new without giving us a map.

If this book helped you feel even a little less alone, then it has already done what it was meant to do.

You don't need to heal perfectly.
You don't need to have everything figured out.
You don't need to rush your becoming.

You are allowed to take this one breath, one moment, one day at a time.

And if no one has told you lately:
> I'm proud of you for showing up for your healing.
> I'm proud of you for staying open.
> I'm proud of you for continuing to live.

Your story still matters.
Your life still holds meaning.
And who you are becoming is worthy of patience and love.

Thank you for letting me walk beside you for a part of your journey.

Take a quiet moment with these questions. There's no right way to answer them. Let honesty guide you.

You may want to journal, reflect silently, or return to these over time.

- What part of this book resonated with me the most?
- What have I learned about myself through grief?
- What feels different about me now compared to when I first started reading?
- What does thriving mean to me today?
- What do I want to carry forward from this experience?
- What am I ready to release?
- Who am I becoming?

You don't need big answers.

Small truths are powerful.

Now, Let's affirm our future together.

You can read these slowly. Out loud if you'd like. Or return to them whenever you need grounding.

- I am allowed to feel everything I feel.
- I am allowed to heal in my own time.
- I am not broken — I am becoming.
- My grief is valid, and so is my joy.
- I don't have to rush my healing.
- I am learning how to live again.
- My body deserves kindness.
- My heart deserves patience.
- My story matters.

- I am allowed to set boundaries.
- I am allowed to grow without guilt.
- I am allowed to dream again.
- I am worthy of peace.
- I am worthy of support.
- I am worthy of a full life.
- Thriving is not something I earn.
- **Thriving is my birthright.**

Acknowledgements

To my children,

Thank you for your love, your patience, and your strength through everything we've faced together.

There were days I didn't have all the answers, and days I was still learning how to stand again—but you gave me a reason to keep trying.

You have shown me what resilience looks like in real life, not in perfection, but in continuing forward even when things are hard.

I am so proud of who you are and who you are becoming.

This book may carry my words, but it is shaped by the life we've lived together and the love that continues to hold us.

You carry so much of your father's love within you, and through you, he remains a part of our everyday lives in ways that words can't fully explain.

And to my husband—your presence continues in the love we share, in our children, and in the strength we've had to find along the way.

You are not forgotten.

I love you, always.

Acknowledgements

This book was born from lived experience, quiet resilience, and countless moments of rebuilding.

I want to acknowledge every person who has walked beside me through seasons of loss — whether through presence, prayer, listening, or simply allowing me to be exactly where I was. Your support mattered more than you know.

To the professionals, therapists, counselors, educators, and healers whose research and compassion continue to shape how we understand grief and trauma — thank you for helping turn pain into knowledge and survival into healing.

To those who have shared their stories with me, trusted me with their grief, and allowed their vulnerability to inspire these pages — I carry your courage with deep respect.

And to you, the reader.

Thank you for choosing yourself.
Thank you for being here.
Thank you for allowing this book into your healing journey.

May you move gently.
May you feel supported.
May you remember that thriving after loss is possible.

Author's Bio

Ceaira Harris is an author, entrepreneur, and grief-informed wellness guide who writes about healing, identity, and rebuilding life after loss. Her work is rooted in lived experience, trauma psychology, and a deep commitment to helping others move beyond survival and into meaningful living.

Having navigated multiple forms of grief — including pregnancy loss, family deaths, sudden violence, widowhood, and the quiet losses that reshape identity — Ceaira understands firsthand how deeply grief affects the nervous system, body, emotions, relationships, and sense of safety in the world.

She writes with compassion, honesty, and grounded psychology, offering readers practical tools for emotional regulation, nervous system healing, and holistic recovery after loss.

Through her writing and work, Ceaira helps people reconnect with themselves, release stored grief, and rediscover hope — not by erasing what they've lost, but by learning how to carry it differently.

Her mission is simple: to remind others that grief is not weakness, healing is not betrayal, and thriving after loss is possible.

Before you go…
**If this book supported you in any way — even in a small, quiet
moment — I would be deeply grateful if you left an honest review.**

Your words don't have to be perfect.
A few sentences about your experience is more than enough.

**Reviews help this book reach other people who are navigating loss
and searching for something that understands what they're going
through.**

You can leave a review directly on Amazon under this book.

Thank you for spending this time with me.
— Ceaira

www.ingramcontent.com/pod-product-compliance
Lightning Source LLC
Chambersburg PA
CBHW060543160726
47991CB00001B/431